From Two Cultures
To No Culture

For Claire Fox
and those who are fighting
the battle of ideas

From Two Cultures
To No Culture

C.P. Snow's 'Two Cultures' Lecture
Fifty Years On

Frank Furedi, Roger Kimball,
Raymond Tallis, Robert Whelan

Civitas: Institute for the Study of Civil Society
London
Registered Charity No. 1085494

First Published March 2009

© Civitas 2009

Civitas is a registered charity (no. 1085494)
and a company limited by guarantee, registered in
England and Wales (no. 04023541)

email: books@civitas.org.uk

ISBN 978-1-906837-04-4
Independence: Civitas: Institute for the Study of Civil
Society is a registered educational charity (No. 1085494) and
a company limited by guarantee (No. 04023541). Civitas is
financed from a variety of private sources to avoid over-
reliance on any single or small group of donors.

All publications are independently refereed. All the Institute's
publications seek to further its objective of promoting the
advancement of learning. The views expressed are those of
the authors, not of the Institute.

Typeset by
Civitas

Printed in Great Britain by
The Cromwell Press Group Ltd
Trowbridge, Wiltshire

The perception of truth is almost as simple a feeling as the perception of beauty; and the genius of Newton, of Shakespeare, of Michael Angelo, and of Handel, are not very remote in character from each other. Imagination, as well as the reason, is necessary to perfection in the philosophic mind. A rapidity of combination, a power of perceiving analogies, and of comparing them by facts, is the creative source of discovery.

Sir Humphry Davy, 1778-1829,
President of the Royal Society

The perennially cited difficulties with the 'two cultures' ... can no longer be accepted... The old rigid debates and boundaries — science versus religion, science versus the arts, science versus traditional ethics — are no longer enough. We should be impatient with them. We need a wider, more generous, more imaginative perspective. Above all, perhaps, we need the three things that a scientific culture can sustain: the sense of individual wonder, the power of hope, and the vivid but questing *belief in a future for the globe.*

Richard Holmes
The Age of Wonder, 2008

Contents

Authors

Frank Furedi is Professor of Sociology at the University of Kent in Canterbury. His research is oriented towards the study of the impact of precautionary culture and risk aversion on Western societies. In his books he has explored controversies and panics over issues such as health, children, food and cultural life. His writings express a concern with the prevailing regime of cultural confusion towards valuing intellectual and artistic pursuits and with the difficulty that society has in providing a challenging education for children and young people. His books include: *Politics of Fear: Beyond Left and Right* (2005); *Where Have All the Intellectuals Gone? Confronting 21st Century Philistinism* (2005); *Therapeutic Culture: Cultivating Vulnerability in an Anxious Age* (2004); *Culture of Fear* (2002); *Paranoid Parenting* (2001); and *Invitation to Terror* (2007). His new book *Lost in Education* will be published in 2009.

Roger Kimball is co-editor and publisher of *The New Criterion* and president and publisher of Encounter Books. He contributes to many periodicals and newspapers in the United States and the UK and writes a regular column for PajamasMedia at http://pajamasmedia.com/rogerkimball. He lectures widely and is the author of several books, including *The Rape of the Masters: How Political Correctness Sabotages Art; Lives of The Mind: The Use and Abuse of Intelligence from Hegel to Wodehouse* (Ivan R. Dee, 2002); *The Long March: How the Cultural Revolution of the 1960s Changed America* (Encounter Books, 2000); and *Tenured Radicals: How Politics Has Corrupted Our Higher Education,* a new edition of which was published in 2008.

Raymond Tallis was Professor of Geriatric Medicine at the University of Manchester from 1988 to 2006. He was elected

x

Fellow of the Academy of Sciences for his research into stroke, epilepsy and neurological rehabilitation. He has honorary degrees of Doctor of Letters from the Universities of Hull (1998) and Manchester (2002) for his writings on philosophy, literature and cultural criticism. His most recent books are *The Enduring Significance of Parmenides: Unthinkable Thought* (Continuum, 2007); *The Kingdom of Infinite Space* (Atlantic, 2008); and *Hunger* (Acumen, 2008). He is the author of two volumes of poetry and his investigation into pointing, *Michelangelo's Finger*, is to be published by Atlantic in 2009.

Robert Whelan is the deputy director of Civitas. His publications include *The Corrosion of Charity* (1996); *Octavia Hill and the Social Housing Debate* (ed.) (1998); *Wild In Woods: The Myth of the Noble Eco-Savage* (1999); *Involuntary Action: How Voluntary is the 'Voluntary' Sector?* (1999); and *Helping the Poor: Friendly Visiting, Dole Charities and Dole Queues* (2001). His edition of *Octavia Hill's Letters to Fellow-Workers, 1872-1911*, co-edited with Anne Anderson, was published in 2005, and he also edited *The Corruption of the Curriculum* in 2007. He is managing director of the New Model School Company, set up by supporters of Civitas in 2003 to bring independent schooling within the reach of more parents, and he teaches English to Bengali students at a Saturday school in London's East End.

Acknowledgements

One of the reasons for the longevity of the debate surrounding C.P. Snow's lecture 'The Two Cultures and the Scientific Revolution' has been the extremely high calibre of his respondents. Whatever one might say of F.R. Leavis's attack on grounds of etiquette, there is little doubt that as an example of incendiary and vituperative prose it is outstanding. Leavis was himself answered in the elegant, measured tones of Lionel Trilling, one of the great twentieth-century essayists. I am therefore deeply grateful to Roger Kimball and Raymond Tallis for allowing me to reprint their very fine contributions to the debate, first published in 1994 and 1995 respectively, and to Frank Furedi for bringing us up to date on the education debate with his characteristically perceptive analysis.

I have been greatly assisted in my attempts to grasp the history of science and society's attitudes towards it by the publication of two superb books in 2008, covering what are sometimes described as the first and second scientific revolutions: *The Phoenix: St Paul's Cathedral and the Men who Made Modern London* by Leo Hollis (Weidenfeld and Nicholson) and *The Age of Wonder: How the Romantic Generation Discovered the Beauty and Terror of Science* by Richard Holmes (HarperPress).

Finally I must gratefully acknowledge my indebtedness to Stefan Collini's excellent introduction to the current Cambridge University Press edition of the *The Two Cultures*, which puts the lecture and the debate that followed into historical and biographical context, with a wealth of fascinating detail.

Robert Whelan

Introduction:
Any Culture At All Would Be Nice

Robert Whelan

On 7 May 1959 the celebrated novelist C.P. Snow mounted the podium in the Senate House, Cambridge to deliver that year's Rede Lecture. He spoke to the title 'The Two Cultures and the Scientific Revolution', taking as his theme the dangerously wide gap that had opened up between scientists and 'literary intellectuals' (representing the humanities) who could now no longer talk to each other. He spoke of scientists who could scarcely struggle through a novel by Dickens, and of literary intellectuals who were ignorant of the Second Law of Thermodynamics.[i]

Snow was not, however, impartial in describing this polarisation. He soon made it clear who were to be regarded as the villains in his scenario: the literary intellectuals who sneered at science as an inferior branch of learning that no really cultured person needed to trouble with, so that ignorance of science did not really count as ignorance at all. He made a series of comparisons between literary intellectuals and scientists that were highly unfavourable to the former, and which boiled down to the claim that, while literary intellectuals are 'natural Luddites', forever mourning the passing of the good old days and digging in their heels

---

[i] The Second Law of Thermodynamics states that energy and matter move toward disorder and overall entropy increases. This Law, having hitherto escaped the limelight of celebrity, was dragged into the public consciousness by Snow to the extent that 'it even featured in a comic song by Flanders and Swan included in their collection *At The Drop of Another Hat*'. (Collini, p. lvii)

1

against progress, scientists had the future in their bones: 'If the scientists have the future in their bones, then the traditional culture responds by wishing the future did not exist.'[1]

He cited the hostility towards the industrial revolution of people like William Morris and John Ruskin, who wanted to turn the clock back to mediaeval craft guilds whilst failing to appreciate the extent to which the changes had transformed the lives of poor people for the better. And if the intellectuals, or the representatives of the 'traditional culture', couldn't cope with the industrial revolution, what could be expected of them in relation to the scientific revolution, which Snow defined as:

> ...the application of real science to industry, no longer hit and miss, no longer the ideas of odd 'inventors', but the real stuff... I believe the industrial society of electronics, atomic energy, automation, is in cardinal respects different in kind from any that has gone before.[2]

Meanwhile, the literary intellectuals don't know what a machine tool is, and pride themselves on their ignorance.

These Luddite tendencies, according to Snow, had political as well as cultural consequences. He accuses literary intellectuals of holding views on questions of government that are not only old-fashioned ('opinions that would have been thought distinctly uncivilised... at the time of the Plantagenets') but 'wicked'. Citing a selection of early twentieth-century writers like Yeats, Pound and Wyndham Lewis who paved the way for Fascist dictators, Snow asks: 'Didn't the influence of all they represent bring Auschwitz that much nearer?'[3] As a loyal man of the Left, Snow neglected to cite George Bernard Shaw and (his especial hero) H.G. Wells whose support for Soviet communism helped to bring Stalin's purges nearer, and in any case Auschwitz was not a happy example for Snow as it represented the use of science, or at least technology, devoid of the moral framework which a liberal and humane education seeks to supply. However, the point could be made even more forcefully half a century later that the most appalling tyrants of the twentieth century all had their coteries of supporters amongst Western intellectuals.

Snow attributed the problem of the two cultures to failures in education. He compared Britain unfavourably with the USA and the USSR, in terms of numbers of young people who remained in education to the age of 18 and above, and in terms of the breadth of the curriculum. He believed (probably correctly) that the British system forced children to specialise at an unusually early age, and that snobbery dictated that the brightest children would be pushed towards the 'traditional culture' and the professions, rather than science and industry, with unfortunate consequences for our international competitiveness: 'If our ancestors had invested talent in the industrial revolution instead of the Indian Empire, we might be more soundly based now. But they didn't.'[4] Snow ended this section of his lecture with a comparison of Britain in his own day with Venice in its decadence:

> Like us, [the Venetians] had once been fabulously lucky. They had become rich, as we did, by accident... They knew, just as clearly as we know, that the current of history had begun to flow against them. Many of them gave their minds to working out ways to keep going. It would have meant breaking the pattern into which they had crystallised. They were fond of the pattern, just as we are fond of ours. They never found the will to break it.[5]

This is an extraordinarily close echo of the famous opening passage of *The Stones of Venice* by John Ruskin—an author Snow despised. But whereas Ruskin saw decline reflected in art and architecture, for Snow it was all about the failure to train enough scientists.

Roughly, if we compare like with like, and put scientists and engineers together, we are training at a professional level per head of the population one Englishman to every one-and-a-half Americans to every two-and-a-half Russians. Someone is wrong.[6]

With Britain condemned by Snow to the slow slide into Venetian decadence, the contest would be between the USA and the USSR. In the final section of his talk, Snow left no doubt about which horse he was backing.

The rich and the poor

In the published version of his speech, Snow called the final section 'The rich and the poor'. This had been his original title for the speech, and he later said that he regretted changing it. In this section Snow looked at the consequences, on an international scale, of the failure to teach science or value scientists properly.

Snow believed that there were 'three menaces' threatening the world: the H-bomb, overpopulation and the gap between the rich and the poor. He says nothing specific about the first two (one of which was, in any case, caused by scientists) but he expatiates at length on the growing gap between the rich inhabitants of the world's developed countries and the rest of the global population. Snow took the view that the growth of inequality would prove to be insupportable in a world of mass communications, in which poor people are aware of the standard of living enjoyed by rich people.

> Whatever else in the world we know survives to the year 2000, that won't. Once the trick of getting rich is known, as it now is, the world can't survive half rich and half poor. It's just not on.[7]

The 'trick' was science. All poor people had to do was adopt Western science and technology, industrialise and make lots of money. And the West would, of course, help them. Only two things were required. First, the transfer of

4

large sums of capital to get the economies of less developed countries beyond a certain point on the industrial curve at which they would be able to accumulate capital. Second, thousands of scientists who would be expected to volunteer for ten years at a time to go to third-world countries, teach them science, then come home filled with the manly pride that comes from the sense of a job well done.

There was just one problem here, from the West's point of view, which was that we didn't produce enough scientists to have them to spare, whereas:

> ...the Russians have a clear edge. This is where their educational policy has already paid big dividends... though I don't know how we can do what we need to do, or whether we shall do anything at all, I do know this: that if we don't do it, the Communist countries will.[8]

In Snow's optimistic world view, 'the task of totally industrialising a major country' was a piece of cake.

> It only takes will to train enough scientists and engineers and technicians. Will, and quite a small number of years. There is no evidence that any country or race is better than any other in scientific teachability... Tradition and technical background seem to count for surprisingly little.[9]

Making predictions is a risky business, and aspiring prophets would be well advised to put the date of fulfilment sufficiently far ahead to ensure they will not be around to see it, as Snow did. In the half-century since this speech, the gap between rich and poor has not vanished, and has probably increased, in spite of the fact that Snow's two conditions have been met. International programmes of foreign aid, that scarcely existed in 1959, have transferred billions upon billions of dollars to third-world governments to get them beyond that elusive point on the curve of economic growth at which they would become capable of generating capital. Many foreign aid programmes have been specifically tied to the transfer of science and technology. Experts from the West have been sent to live and work in the third world courtesy of huge supra-national bodies such as the United Nations, the World Bank and their agencies. However, the forces of 'tradition and technical background' that Snow dismissed so airily have proved to be real. At the end of the Second World War, both South East Asia and sub-Saharan Africa were in severe economic difficulties. The countries of South East Asia, which received comparatively small amounts of foreign aid, made such remarkable progress on world markets that Western nations were reduced to calling for trade barriers to protect their home industries from 'unfair' competition. Many of the countries of sub-Saharan Africa, on the other hand, have actually gone into economic reverse, with citizens experiencing a lower quality of life than pertained at the time of their independence from the European colonial powers. It turns out that there is more to closing the gap between rich and poor than transferring funds and sending a few boffins on overseas missions.

Snow's anticipation of the triumph of Soviet science proved to be equally wide of the mark. The USSR never came anywhere near equalling the scientific achievements of the USA. The Soviets lost the space race and the development of Star Wars technology by the USA was one of the factors that precipitated the collapse of communism. Much of the USSR's technology was simply stolen from the West. As for Russia's selfless sharing of the benefits of progress with the third world while the Western nations skulked in the background—well, it must have seemed a charming fantasy in the Cambridge of 1959.

The sorcerer's apprentice

Critics of Snow's 'Two Cultures' speech usually focus on this last section where history has falsified many of his predictions, but of course Snow's original audience could have known nothing of this. He was a highly respected cultural commentator whose broad range of experience and high-level connections caused many people to regard him as a man whose opinions deserved to be taken seriously. However, no one could have predicted the extent of the debate that 'The Two Cultures' provoked.

The lecture was published in pamphlet form, then it appeared in two issues of *Encounter*.[10] According to Snow, he expected the matter to end there. In fact, the global response was overwhelming, with articles and debates in countries around the world in which Snow had never been published before: 'By the end of the year I began to feel uncomfortably like the Sorcerer's Apprentice.'[11] But the most astounding response to Snow's lecture was still to come. In 1962 F.R. Leavis, the literary critic and *eminence grise* of the Cambridge English faculty, chose to use the 1962 Richmond Lecture at Downing College, which he was invited to deliver just before retiring as Reader in English, to pass judgment on Snow's thesis.

Leavis's lecture was so astonishingly vitriolic, seasoned with an almost toxic dose of the most vulgar *ad hominem* abuse, that, when I was an undergraduate in the English faculty ten years later, people were still talking about it in tones of shock and awe. Leavis began by criticising the confident tone of Snow's lecture—'a tone of which one can say that, while only genius could justify it, one cannot readily think of genius adopting it'.[12(ii)] He went on to assure the audience that:

(ii) Snow had first explored his Two Cultures thesis in an article for the *New Statesman* (6 October 1956) in which he described scientists as, on the whole, manly, heterosexual types, unlike the literary intellectuals who tend to be 'feline and oblique'. The tone Leavis

Not only is [Snow] not a genius, he is intellectually as undistinguished as it is possible to be... Snow... is, in himself, negligible... 'The Two Cultures' exhibits an utter lack of intellectual distinction and an embarrassing vulgarity of style... the lecture was conceived and written by someone who had not had the advantage of an intellectual discipline of any kind... He knows nothing of history. He pronounces about it with as complete a confidence as he pronounces about literature... but he is equally ignorant of both... Snow rides on an advancing swell of cliché: this exhilarating motion is what he takes for inspired and authoritative thought.[13]

There was a great deal more in this vein, and one wonders what the effect of it must have been on that original audience gathered at Downing, listening to an attack on a living and respected member of the University of such unprecedented ferocity. Leavis was criticised, in the immediate aftermath of the speech and right down to the present day, for the vitriolic tone of his attack. It was, as Lionel Trilling wrote in an assessment that appeared later in the year, 'a bad tone, an impermissible tone'.[14] There was (and is) a feeling that it should have been possible to make whatever points he had in disagreement with Snow without letting loose such a fusillade of personal abuse. However, Leavis's view was that the thesis of 'Two Cultures' had become pervasive exactly because of the sort of man Snow was, and that *ad hominem* abuse was therefore of the essence.

Snow had trained as a scientist and enjoyed a brief career as a research scientist at Cambridge before devoting himself full-time to writing. During the Second World War Snow had held an important position, recruiting scientists for the Civil Service to work in the war effort. During the war he

adopted in his lecture seemed to prove Snow's point: the claws were certainly out. The most poisonous old queen of the Footlights could not have bettered some of Leavis's devastating put-downs.

began the series of novels that became known as *Strangers and Brothers*, eventually running to 11 volumes and enjoying great success, including a series of stage adaptations. *Strangers and Brothers* followed the career of Lewis Elliot (Snow's thinly veiled self-portrait) from humble provincial beginnings to the very top of the establishment, pacing the Corridors of Power—a phrase which Snow invented and which became the title of one of the novels. Snow was therefore seen by many people as being ideally placed to speak of the gulf opening up between the two cultures of science and the arts because he had a foot in both camps. To discredit his thesis, Leavis had to show that Snow's foothold was a very loose one, at least in the world of literature.

F.R. Leavis was one of the most influential literary critics of the twentieth century. He transformed the way in which literature was understood and evaluated by insisting on the moral seriousness of great literature, and its ability to act as a formative influence on individuals and society. He was not interested in any literature that was not great. In fact, his hostility towards those who purveyed second-rate literature was probably greater than the contempt he felt for people who had nothing to do with books at all.[iii] Leavis had made a special study of the English novel in his book *The Great Tradition* that reduced the number of English-language novelists worth reading to a mere handful. He regarded a feebly written novel as an almost personal affront.

It is for this reason that, as Stefan Collini put it in his introduction to the Cambridge University Press edition of

---

[iii] Leavis cherished an especial contempt for the Sunday newspapers, which he thought represented all that was worst in a trivialised and degraded culture.

the lecture: '...a malevolent deity, setting out to design a single figure in whom the largest number of Leavis's deepest antipathies would find themselves embodied could not have done better than to create Charles Percy Snow'.[15] Snow's novels had enjoyed both commercial and critical success, but Leavis regarded them as utter trash:

> Snow is, of course, a—no, I can't say that; he isn't: Snow thinks of himself as a novelist... as a novelist he doesn't exist; he doesn't begin to exist. He can't be said to know what a novel is. The nonentity is apparent on every page of his fictions... I am trying to remember where I heard (can I have dreamed it?) that they are composed for him by an electronic brain called Charlie, into which instructions are fed in the form of chapter headings... Snow not only hasn't in him the beginnings of a novelist; he is utterly without a glimmer of what creative literature is, or why it matters.[16]

This made it all the more galling for Leavis that Snow, largely on the basis of his novels (his scientific career had not been hugely successful[(iv)]), was accepted as a sage, a man whose views on any subject could command a hearing. Leavis, on the other hand, had always struggled for recognition, despite believing himself to represent 'the essential Cambridge in spite of Cambridge'.[17] He was appointed Reader in English only three years before his retirement in the year of his Richmond lecture, and Sir Arthur Quiller Couch, who supervised the young Leavis's

---

[(iv)] Appointed a fellow of Christ's College, Cambridge in 1930, at the age of only 25, Snow's career as a research scientist suffered a major setback two years later when he and a colleague announced that they discovered the method to synthesise Vitamin A. The announcement received considerable publicity, but unfortunately they were soon to receive even more publicity when they discovered that the calculations were faulty and the claim had to be retracted.

PhD thesis, had written privately in 1924, when Leavis was struggling to establish himself in an academic career, that his young pupil's 'self-sufficiency' would mean that 'no good fortune would easily equal his sense of his deserts'.[18] This accounts, in part at least, for the 'impermissible tone' of his attack on Snow.

Leavis's lecture was reprinted in the *Spectator* on 9 March 1962, and later in the year in book form by Chatto and Windus. Both publishers, seeking to avoid an action for libel, contacted Snow to ask if he required any changes in the text. As Snow himself observed in his 1963 lecture to the Royal Institution 'The Two Cultures and the Sorcerer's Apprentice', it is a fairly extraordinary state of affairs when academic disputes reach the limits of the law of defamation; but to his eternal credit he said that the text should be published as it stood.

The question is, why did he do so? According to Philip Snow's biography of his famous brother, he was deeply distressed by the attack and the unpleasantness of the publicity that ensued, to the extent that he became a less jovial figure after 1962—'the year of trauma'.[19] He seriously considered bringing an action for libel and was certainly no stranger to this method of defending his reputation. He had been the plaintiff in several cases which had been settled out of court, including one against *Private Eye* which had run a piece claiming that he had taken the whole Swedish Academy out to dinner to increase his chance of winning the Nobel Prize for Literature.[v] This was clearly a joke, as Snow

---

[v] *Private Eye*, which had a track record for abusing Snow as C P Snurd, Sir Charles Snurd and finally Lord Snurd, had made matters worse while Snow's case was in progress by including him in a list of names from which readers were asked to select the ugliest man in Britain (3 February 1965). The magazine had to pay

was known to be desperate to get the prize, but he was presumably still suffering from the sense-of-humour failure occasioned by the 'year of trauma' and failed to see the funny side.[20]

So why did Snow not sue Leavis? It would be nice to think that his writer's love of words gave him some satisfaction in being the cause of such a baroque outpouring of abuse as had scarcely been heard since the *saeva indignatio* of Jonson and Swift, or the denunciation of Oscar Wilde's immorality by the Solicitor-General at the Old Bailey, 'like a thing out of Tacitus, like a passage in Dante, like one of Savonarola's indictments of the Popes at Rome'.[21] Unfortunately Snow did not really have that feeling for language. (Leavis was far from being the only critic to comment on the flat prose style of Snow's novels, although his claim that they were composed by an electronic brain called Charlie was somewhat far-fetched.)

Perhaps Snow felt that, whatever the hurt to his personal feelings, Leavis's contribution would keep the debate going. If so, he was right. Almost immediately, starting with Lionel Trilling's brilliant essay that appeared in *Commentary* later in the same year,[22] the dispute became known as the Snow/ Leavis controversy (or sometimes, no doubt gallingly for Snow, the Leavis/Snow controversy). It has been turned over and pulled apart by commentators from all points on the academic and political compass for nearly half a century. There can be little doubt that Snow's 'Two Cultures' lecture was one of the most stimulating contributions to public debate delivered in such a format during the twentieth century.

£200 in damages and undertake not to mention Snow again—an undertaking that was almost immediately broken.

However, Snow was realistic enough to acknowledge that when a debate takes on a global dimension as quickly as his lecture did, it means that the idea is not new. People must have been thinking about it before, so that the lecture acted as the spark to ignite a debate that was waiting to happen. The strange thing is that Snow appeared not to realise just what a distinguished history, close to home in Cambridge, the controversy had enjoyed in the previous century.

Two cultures—the prequel

Stefan Collini has told the story of a prequel to the Snow/Leavis (or arts *vs* science) controversy that involved another Rede Lecture in 1882, 77 years before Snow mounted the same platform. The Rede Lecturer on this occasion was Matthew Arnold, son of Dr Arnold of Rugby School, poet and pre-eminent Victorian man of letters. His title was 'Literature and Science', and he discussed whether or not the traditional classical education of *literae humaniores* was still relevant in an age of great scientific and technical advance. He decided that it was; while scientific knowledge had its own value in practical application, no one could be really educated unless he (it was inevitably 'he') understood literature, particularly the literature of ancient Greece and Rome.[23] Arnold was responding to an earlier lecture by T.H. Huxley, known as Darwin's Bulldog for his rumbustious defence of the Theory of Evolution, given at the opening of a science college in Birmingham. Huxley (who took the Snow part in this exchange) argued that science was as valid an intellectual training as the classics and deserved a more prominent place in the school curriculum.[24]

This Huxley/Arnold prequel (conducted in terms of the greatest courtesy as the two men were friends) to the Snow/Leavis bust-up may give the impression that scholars have been arguing about this since the days of Aristotle, but in fact the idea of separating academic disciplines into groups known as science and humanities (or *literae humaniores* or the traditional culture or the arts) was no older than the century in which Arnold and Huxley were conducting their gentlemanly exchange.

For hundreds of years, every branch of learning had been regarded as a science. In the middle ages theology was the Queen of the Sciences, and in his 1755 *Dictionary of the English Language* Samuel Johnson defined science as: 'any art or species of knowledge'. Johnson, the Great Cham[vi] of eighteenth-century letters, was a keen amateur scientist who performed experiments in chemistry in a little laboratory in the attic of his house,[vii] while Alexander Pope, the poetic voice of Augustan England, wrote the famous couplet:

Nature and Nature's laws lay hid in night;
God said, 'Let Newton be!' —and all was light.

'Science is the great antidote to the poison of enthusiasm and superstition'[25] wrote Adam Smith in *The Wealth of Nations*, and there was no conflict between arts and sciences for the Georgians, who still lived at a time when it was supposed that an educated person ought to know at least something about all of the major branches of learning. However, the Romantic movement that emerged towards the end of the eighteenth century represented a fundamental shift in the way in which people came to regard themselves and their relations with both human society and with the natural world. Amongst other things, this caused a certain hostility to

---

[vi] The soubriquet was first awarded by Tobias Smollett in a letter to John Wilkes dated 16 March 1759.

[vii] In his *Dictionary*, Johnson defined a chemist as 'a philosopher by fire'.

emerge towards science, which was felt to be draining everything that was beautiful and mysterious and transcendental from the universe. 'Art is the Tree of Life, Science is the Tree of Death' wrote William Blake, [26] while Coleridge declared of atheistical French science, which elevated reason above religion and morality, that: 'We have purchased a few brilliant inventions at the loss of all communion with life and the spirit of nature'.[27]

In his account of the Romantics and their relationship with science, *The Age of Wonder*, Richard Holmes argues that the supposed hostility of the Romantic poets towards science has been much exaggerated, and can largely be blamed on a much-quoted account of a dinner given in 1817 by the painter Benjamin Haydon to celebrate the completion of the first stage of his enormous canvas *Christ's Entry into Jerusalem*. The guests included William Wordsworth, Charles Lamb and John Keats and:

> During the increasingly rowdy dinner-table discussion that developed, the painting provoked a debate about the powers of Reason versus the Imagination. The destructive and reductive effects of the scientific outlook were mocked. Warming to the theme, Lamb mischievously described Newton as 'a fellow who believed nothing unless it was as clear as the three sides of a triangle'. Keats joined in, agreeing that Newton had 'destroyed all the poetry of the rainbow, by reducing it to a prism'. Haydon jovially records: 'It was impossible to resist them, and we drank "Newton's health, and confusion to Mathematics".' [28]

We should beware of attaching too much weight to the banter of a few bibulous poets in their cups, and there is a danger of over-simplifying enormously complex cultural movements by taking a few quotations out of context. As Richard Holmes points out, Keats, as a medical student, had enough science to know that these observations on Newton were idiotic,[viii] and the conversation might have gone another way with a different guest-list: Haydon was a fundamentalist Christian and would no doubt have encouraged the anti-science toast. The relationship between the Romantics and science was much more layered than the above quotations would suggest, and the Romantics created their own image of the scientist as a lonely, questing individual, going against the grain of the established order, 'voyaging in strange seas of thought alone', as Wordsworth wrote of Newton. Nevertheless, it is clear that a new conception of science as a branch of learning which is of a different nature to the arts was emerging. Furthermore, there was a strong feeling, at least in some quarters, that the technological benefits of scientific research may not be equal to the damage science was doing to people's conception of nature and their place in the natural order.[ix] It is not co-incidental that Mary Shelley, wife of the great Romantic poet Percy Bysshe Shelley, created the character who has become synonymous with the concept of science that is dangerous and out-of-control: Dr Frankenstein.[x][29]

[viii] This did not stop Keats from returning to his lament for the lost mysteries of the rainbow in 'Lamia': 'There was an awful rainbow once in heaven:/ We know her woof, her texture; she is given/ In the dull catalogue of common things./ Philosophy will clip an Angel's wings.' (Lines 231-34, quoted in Holmes, p. 323.)

[ix] 'The progress of science', wrote Carlyle in *Sartor Resartus* (1833) 'is to destroy wonder, and in its stead substitute mensuration and numeration.' (Quoted in Holmes, p. 436.)

[x] As Richard Holmes points out, although Victor Frankenstein has come to represent 'the archetypal mad and evil scientist... in the original novel he is also a romantic and idealistic figure' (p. 335). However, decadence, that curious cultural phenomenon of the last part of the nineteenth century, produced a reaction against the

What is undeniable is that, from the early decades of the nineteenth century, the arts and sciences went their separate ways, and 'science' came to be used to describe only those studies relating to the physical or experimental sciences. The term 'scientist' was coined at their 1833 meeting in Cambridge by members of the British Association for the Advancement of Science who were concerned that there was no term specifically to describe 'students of the knowledge of the material world... some ingenious gentleman proposed that, by analogy with *artist*, they might form *scientist*'. The name stuck.[30]

With arts and science now occupying separate camps, the battle for control of the school curriculum could begin. There was no problem about mathematics, which had been at the core of the classical curriculum for hundreds of years, but there was a definite unwillingness to take valuable class-

---

scientific method which was much less ambivalent than any reservations entertained by the Romantic poets. In *Là-bas* (1891), a lip-smacking novel of Satanism and child abuse, arch-decadent J.K. Huysmans makes frequent comparisons between the sterility and bankruptcy of science and the superiority of the good old ways of magic, astrology and Black Masses. The German author Max Nordau wrote a famous attack on decadence called *Degeneration* (1892) in which he excoriated decadents for their claims that science had deceived us and broken her promises. 'When has she ever promised anything else than honest and attentive observation of phenomena and, if possible, establishment of the conditions under which they occur? ... If anyone has expected of her that she would explain from one day to another the whole mechanism of the universe, like a juggler explains his apparent magic, he has no idea of the true mission of science.' (p. 107 of the English translation published by Heinemann in 1920.)

room time from Virgil and Homer and give it to physics and chemistry. [xi]

Make stinks for fun

The low status of science in the education system that Huxley complained of in 1880 and that Snow complained of in 1959 was real enough. In 1945 John Moore published his autobiographical *Portrait of Elmbury*, about growing up in Tewkesbury in Gloucestershire in the early 1900s. He describes his education in a prep school where he comes under the influence of Mr Chorlton, the Latin master. The young John Moore wrecks the classroom by mixing chemicals together to see if they will explode. As it is his last term, the headmaster, instead of beating him black and blue, hands his punishment over to Mr Chorlton, who asks him if

---

[xi] There were some noble exceptions: 'One of the very first people to introduce the teaching of natural science into English classrooms was Rev. J.M. Wilson who was one of the first teachers of science at Rugby. In an anthology on the nature of a liberal education, published in 1867, Wilson explained the intrinsic benefits that are uniquely obtainable from having acquired even a basic scientific understanding of the world: "Scientific knowledge… is no mean, and peddling, and quibbling knowledge, as the ignorant believe; it is the key to the highest ideas… The great thoughts and principles which are to be gained by scientific knowledge are not only of a quality that increases the dignity of a man's mind… but are not inferior… to those which may be reached by other studies… To [someone who has gained the benefits of a scientific education], the stars of heaven, and the stones of earth, the forms of the hills, and the flowers of the hedges, are a constant source of that great and peculiar pleasure derived from intelligence."' [David Conway, 'Save our Science', Civitas blog, 2 December 2008. www.civitas.org.uk]

he was performing a serious experiment or just trying to cause an explosion. He decides to be honest and says he just wanted the explosion, to which Mr Chorlton replies: 'Good. I was afraid you might have had some serious scientific purpose. If so I'd have beaten you. The educational value of chemistry is almost exactly equal to that of a jigsaw. Make stinks for fun, but if you want to learn things, stick to Virgil.'[31] That was the tradition in which I was educated in the 1960s at a school in which the bright boys were expected to read classics at Oxford while the less bright boys were steered towards the labs; and the Nobel Prize-winning scientist Sir Andrew Huxley recounts that, when he switched from classics to physics, the headmaster of Westminster School accused him of 'forsaking virtue for pleasure'.[32]

Snow seems to have regarded his 'Two Cultures' lecture as being primarily about education. 'There is only one way out of all this', he wrote; 'it is, of course, by rethinking our education.'[33] In his 1963 talk to the Royal Institution, looking back on the controversy, he was still insisting that: 'The chief means open to us is education—education mainly in primary and secondary schools', and he spoke of his surprise at the way in which 'some straightforward proposals about education, intended to be simple and practical, have been made the jumping-off point for a debate on first and last things'.[34]

As many people have pointed out, there are in fact no concrete proposals for education, straightforward or otherwise, in 'The Two Cultures'.[xii] Snow had no professional

---

[xii] Lionel Trilling was so struck by the complete absence of 'a single substantial proposal for education' that he assumed the real purpose of Snow's lecture was geopolitical: to secure peace between the West and the Soviet bloc. (pp. 413 and 414.)

experience of primary or secondary education, and although he complains that pupils specialise too early in Britain compared with other countries, and that not enough continue in education until 18 and beyond, there are no specific remedies suggested. It should be remembered that after Snow's initial even-handedness, complaining of scientists who can't read a novel by Dickens and literary intellectuals who can't define the Second Law of Thermodynamics, Snow has nothing more to say about the need for scientists to broaden their horizons. The emphasis is entirely on the need for greater attention to science, especially in the light of his final analysis of global problems that can only be solved by an enormous increase in the number of scientists available for export to the third world. This could lead to more specialisation in the curriculum, not less.

However, given Snow's stated concern that education, and science education in particular, was central to solving the problems he outlined, it is reasonable to ask, what would he think of the state of science education today?

The corruption of the curriculum

In June 2007 Civitas published a collection of essays under the title *The Corruption of the Curriculum* in which six subject specialists wrote of the way in which their respective subjects were being drained of intellectual content. In many cases, the traditional subjects of the school curriculum have been hollowed out to turn them into vehicles to allow the government to address certain topical concerns. This has given us geography as a vector for environmentalism; history from which all narrative has been stripped out and only politically-correct 'highlights' like slavery and Hitler are insisted upon; and English in which the ethnicity and gender of authors trump the beauty of their prose or verse.

However it was the chapter on science that provided the genesis for the book. 'What is science education for?' by David Perks had already been published as a separate booklet by the Institute of Ideas to considerable acclaim. Perks was writing against the background of a major change in the way in which science education would be delivered, using an approach called Twentieth Century Science, from September 2006. This change was in itself a response to what was perceived as a crisis in science education. Fewer students were taking science at A-level; the majority of science teachers in schools lacked a degree in the relevant subject; university departments of science were closing or being threatened with closure; leaders of industry were complaining that it was becoming so difficult to find good scientists in Britain that they were outsourcing recruitment to China and India; and politicians were aware of the impact of a decline in scientifically qualified workers on international competitiveness.

The new science GCSE was designed to persuade more students to take science at A-level and university by making it more interesting and relevant to their own lives. The three disciplines of chemistry, physics and biology were to be conflated under the heading of 'scientific literacy' and children would be encouraged to discuss topical issues such as global warming and MMR vaccines, with particular reference to media coverage. Perks criticises this approach on several pedagogic levels. It treats science as a branch of media studies, rather than as discrete bodies of knowledge to be transmitted to the student; it assumes that children can relate only to what they know, and that they should not be challenged by new concepts; it gives too much weight to what children say they enjoy, rather than stretching them to develop their capacity for abstract thought; and the controlled laboratory experiment—'the backbone of modern scientific enquiry'—has been replaced by field studies. Perks also objects to the way in which traditional science teaching has been caricatured as the rote-learning of dry and disembodied facts. Science teaching, in his view, should be:

> ... about treating students as potential future scientists and providing them with the foundations of a scientific understanding of the world that will stand them in good stead whether they pursue science further or not.[35]

The great irony associated with the new science GCSE is that it was introduced with the stated intention of giving us a more scientifically literate population, which would increase our international competitiveness, but research published *after* Twentieth Century Science had been rolled out across the country indicated that students are now *less* likely to say that they are interested in science and intend to study science to A-level.[36]

Independent schools are bailing out from the new science GCSE by taking the International GCSE (IGCSE) that still retains the three separate sciences. This is contributing towards what Perks describes as 'educational apartheid', with state-school pupils less likely to read for science degrees at university as they simply won't know enough science. Independent schools could come to dominate university science departments in the same way that they currently dominate language departments, ancient and modern.

This would have appalled C.P. Snow, who came from a lower middle-class background and grew up with few material advantages. He attended the local grammar school in Leicester, which specialised in science, while the local public library opened up the world of imaginative literature to him. He joined the chemistry and physics department at Leicester University College where he obtained a first in chemistry, followed by an MSc. He worked himself to the verge of a nervous breakdown, but succeeded in getting admitted to

Christ's College, Cambridge as a PhD student. He was awarded a fellowship at the comparatively early age of 25.

Such a progress for a bright boy from a poor background would be almost impossible to imagine today, for all sorts of reasons. Most of the grammar schools that provided a ladder out of poverty for bright children from poor families have gone, and the public library would now be crowded with internet surfers and people drinking coffee. The academic rigour that characterised the pedagogy of even those schools catering for poor children is also, alas, largely a thing of the past. Politicians boost examination results by dumbing down the curriculum and awarding high GCSE grades for vocational qualifications like hairdressing and tourism, but objective tests have exposed the sleight of hand.[37]

As a result, social mobility is falling in Britain, which comes towards the bottom of the OECD league tables.[38] One indicator of this is the proportion of children from state schools admitted to Oxford and Cambridge, which is lower now than it was in the 1960s,[39] in spite of intense political pressure on the universities from a government desperate to justify its policies.

The problems that now characterise our education system are no respecters of subject boundaries. English dons are confronted by students who have never read a play by Shakespeare right through, and for whom a novel by Henry James would be unimaginably hard. A history don at Cambridge told me he is teaching undergraduates who do not know what the Renaissance and the Reformation were, or which came first. Secondary schools complain that they have to do catch-up when children join them from primary schools. Universities complain that they are having to run foundation courses to teach students the basics of writing an essay.

When I was editing *The Corruption of the Curriculum* I was aware of the danger that always faces editors of multi-author volumes: you sometimes find yourselves with a collection of chapters that don't fit together to make a book. In fact, I had no need to worry, because all of the contributors told the same story. From history to geography, from English to French, subjects have been drained of their academic coherence and rigour. It is more than a case of dumbing down: the school timetable is now seen by politicians as a weapon to deploy in fighting all sorts of battles that have nothing to do with education, from social cohesion and anti-racism to obesity and teenage pregnancy. Boosting self-esteem is more important than telling children which answers are right and which are wrong. The situation is so serious now that it has gone from being a topic for educationalists to debate to an issue of whether or not the culture we have inherited from our parents is going to be passed on to our children. To take a specific but telling example, the disinclination shown by young people to vote in general elections is understandable in the context of a complete failure to teach the history of the development of parliamentary democracy and the free society in Britain.

This is a situation that would have appalled Leavis and Snow equally. As Lionel Trilling pointed out, in spite of their spectacular disagreement over the 'Two Cultures' lecture, they were both 'of the Roundhead party' and had a great deal in common:

> A lively young person of advanced tastes would surely say that
> if ever two men were committed to England, Home and Duty,
> they are Leavis and Snow—he would say that in this they are as
> alike as two squares.[40]

The interesting thing about the campaign run by the Institute of Ideas during 2006 to call attention to the problematic nature of the new science GCSE was that it was cross-disciplinary. At the meetings I attended there were contributions from educationalists working in literature and languages as well as the sciences. The people who worry about children with A* in science GCSE who do not know of the periodic table are the same people who worry about children who think they have 'done' *Macbeth* when they have read two scenes, without knowing how it ends. The old debate between arts and sciences, to which Snow and Leavis gave the most pungent twentieth-century expression, is now completely out of date. It is no longer a question of whether children should be taught to translate Horace or solve algebraic equations: it is a question of whether they are to be taught anything at all with the academic rigour that used to characterise the British education system. In 1959 Snow worried about divisions between the two cultures; we now have to ask ourselves whether our culture can survive, in any meaningful sense, at all.

And as Lionel Trilling said, Leavis and Snow, both committed to England, Home and Duty, would probably find themselves on the same side today, in that respect at least.

The legacy

Is there any point in going over this famous debate again, half-a-century after one of the most explosive exchanges ever to echo throughout the courts of our ancient seats of learning?

I think the answer is yes, because the Snow/Leavis controversy raised the most profound questions about the nature of education and what we expect it to achieve. Snow was right to criticise the supercilious dismissal of science as 'stinks', not fit for gentlemen, when scientific understanding can be both beautiful and vital in the culture. Leavis was right to call attention to the need for science to operate within the framework of moral values that a humane education can generate. The fact that science *permits* us to do certain things doesn't mean that we *should* do them, whether it be the creation of a master race or the creation of animal/human hybrids.

The debate wasn't new in 1959, and it didn't end there either, but the issues were raised to a higher profile than ever before by the skills of the combatants. Whatever Leavis and others might say about the prose style of C.P. Snow's novels, his lecture was beautifully written, designed to enable those possessed of no specialist knowledge to understand and take part in a debate on academic issues which would nowadays almost certainly be wrapped up in impenetrable jargon. Leavis's response was so spectacularly over-the-top that it is impossible not to relish the way in which he handles the language of scurrilous *ad hominem* abuse in a way scarcely seen since the Battle of the Books.[xiii]

There is another reason for revisiting Snow that is touched on by Roger Kimball in a footnote to his essay, and which is explored by Raymond Tallis in *Newton's Sleep*, the

---

[xiii] The Battle of the Books was a dispute over the respective merits of ancient and modern authors that began in France towards the end of the seventeenth century. Fontanelle and others argued that modern authors were better than the ancients because their science has eclipsed the ignorant superstition of past ages. Sir William Temple, former Secretary of State for Charles II, responded in 1690 with his essay *On Ancient and Modern Learning*, arguing that the ancients told us everything we need to know about human nature, and that if the moderns claim to see further, it is because they are dwarves standing on the shoulders of those earlier giants. Jonathan Swift, who was Temple's secretary at the time, later waded into the feud with his short *Battle of the Books* that was prefaced to the first edition of the *Tale of a Tub* in 1704. This envisages a battle taking place between the books in a library fighting for the honour of their respective authors.

book from which his chapter in this book is extracted. The gentlemanly disdain for science that irritated T.H. Huxley in the nineteenth century and C.P. Snow in the twentieth was as nothing to the extraordinary suspicion, amounting to a hatred, of science that emerged from the growth of the Green movement in the 1980s.

Concerns about issues such as the 'hole' in the ozone layer and global warming persuaded many people that man's impact on the planet had become so destructive that we were in danger of an ecological disaster on such as scale as to render the planet uninhabitable by man or any other species. The blame for this potential holocaust was laid at the feet of Western Man who, thanks to his Western culture of science and technology, had impacted the natural order on a scale never before witnessed. At the extreme edges of the Green movement was a profound misanthropy that was directed in particular against the West and its scientific culture, because that culture had enabled more human beings to live on the planet and to dominate nature. The answer, therefore, was a simpler existence, closer to the land.

Some people—the Deep Greens—opted out of modern society altogether, and even adopted terrorist tactics against mainstream consumerist culture. These people were never more than a lunatic fringe, but the idea that science was a problem, and that technological advance had gone far enough, percolated throughout society. Green campaigners who claimed that, if everyone in the world wanted to enjoy an affluent Western lifestyle, the planet faced extinction, found a responsive audience.

In his 1959 lecture Snow said that if intellectual Luddites wanted to turn their backs on the benefits of industrialisation, go hungry, see most of their children die in infancy and lose 20 years off their lifespans, they were free to make that choice, and 'I respect you for the strength of your aesthetic revulsion. But I don't respect you in the slightest if, even passively, you try to impose the same choice on others who are not free to choose.'[41] Unfortunately this is exactly what some Greens have tried to do, and in some cases succeeded in doing. The most egregious example of Green self-righteousness resulting in Third World suffering relates to the banning of DDT.

Since the dawn of human societies, malaria had been one of the greatest plagues. The discovery of DDT just after the Second World War provided the first effective remedy against it. Programmes of spraying were so successful that cases went down to a spectacular degree: in India from an estimated 75 million in 1951 to about 50,000 in 1961; in Sri Lanka from about three million cases just after World War Two to 29 in 1964. However, in 1962 Rachel Carson, who was dying of cancer at the time, published what would become the Magna Carta of the modern environmental movement, *Silent Spring*. She claimed that the earth was being so poisoned by chemicals that rivers would be emptied of fish and birds would disappear from the trees— hence the title. Specifically, DDT was accused of causing the deaths of birds of prey such as the bald eagle (the national bird of the USA) and the peregrine falcon and of causing cancer in humans. There was no evidence to support these charges at the time and they have since been demonstrated to be untrue. Nevertheless, the nascent Green movement got the bit between its teeth and went after DDT as one of the Dirty Dozen chemicals. DDT was banned in the USA in 1972 after a bitter campaign during which the most eminent scientists had declared that there was no evidence to support the case against it. The US National Academy of Science estimated that: 'in a little more than two decades, DDT has prevented 50 million human deaths from malaria' and Philip Handler, the president of the Academy and a distinguished biologist, described DDT as 'the greatest chemical that has ever been discovered'.[42] The ban in the USA meant that American aid could not be used to pay for it, and even if developing countries could find their own funds to purchase the chemical, increasingly tight environmental regulations in Western countries meant that their produce could not be sold on Western markets if it contained traces of the banned substance.

Unsurprisingly, malaria re-emerged on a huge scale. There are now millions of cases and approximately one million malaria-related deaths a year, mostly children. Of course this suffering afflicts people in the Third World with black and brown skins and consequently scarcely figures on the radar of the Green movement, which is white, Western and middle-class. (One suspects that if malaria were to break out in North-West London, DDT would be back in production pdq.) As Dick Taverne puts it: 'if a total ban on DDT worldwide is made effective, it will be a victory for the conscience of the rich world, invoked without regard for the facts, at the expense of the lives of the inarticulate poor'.[43]

Bad as this is, the fear of science and technology has turned into something more than an attempt to limit the spread of their benefits. Science now faces the charge that it is only one way of understanding the world, and not necessarily superior to rival conceptions such as magic and witch-doctors. Science is seen as depending, for its validity, upon such Western concepts as 'proof', 'reason' and even 'truth'. Science is only 'true' when its claims are supported by authority figures in Western societies. Magic may be equally 'true' in traditional societies that look up to witch-doctors.[xiv]

(xiv) Raymond Tallis asks why, 'if scientific discourse has nothing to do with natural reality, streptomycin does and magic does not cure

These claims are not being made by cranks and fringe figures—or perhaps I should say not exclusively by cranks and fringe figures. Some of those who support this interpretation are at the heart of the cultural establishment, including university professors. They show, as Roger Kimball notes in his chapter (p. 38), that 'this new hostility to science is part of a more general hostility to Western values and institutions, an anti-Enlightenment hostility that "mocks the idea that... a civilisation is capable of progressing from ignorance to insight".' This is not an idea that either Snow or Leavis would have wanted to see mocked. Nor would any of the contributors to the present volume. The notion that human beings are capable of moving from barbarism to civilisation by using their intellectual and moral capacities is one that can unite even those who are divided over the respective merits of scientists and literary intellectuals. Which is something.

TB. Is this a question of the mycobacterium being less frightened by the group dynamics of priests than of those of microbiologists?' (p. 58.)

The Two Cultures Today(i)

Roger Kimball

It is not a question of annihilating science, but of controlling it. Science is totally dependent upon philosophical opinions for all of its goals and methods, though it easily forgets this.

Friedrich Nietzsche

[T]he more that the results of science are frankly accepted, the more that poetry and eloquence come to be received and studied as what in truth they really are—the criticism of life by gifted men, alive and active with extraordinary power.

Matthew Arnold

'The corridors of power' and 'The Two Cultures': these phrases are essentially what remain of the once towering reputation of Sir Charles Percy Snow, novelist, pundit and —as his harshest critic, F.R. Leavis, put it—'public relations man' for science. C.P. Snow (1905-1980) was the son of a provincial church organist who rose to public acclaim and a life peerage through a mixture of geniality, application, and talent—more or less in that order. He was the embodiment of a certain type of educated philistine: bluff, well-meaning, clubbable, so well-rounded as to be practically spherical. In the Thirties, Snow abandoned an incipient scientific career in order to devote himself to writing. He published his first novel, a whodunit called *Death Under Sail*, in 1932. During the war, Snow's technical background helped win him the important post of overseeing recruitment for Britain's scientific research (hence his acquaintance with 'the corridors of

---

(i) First published in *The New Criterion*, February 1994. Revised 2000.

power'). And the novels kept appearing. By the Fifties, Snow's novel sequence *Strangers and Brothers* was occasionally compared to *A la recherche du temps perdu*.

Today, the word that seems most often used to describe his novels—on the rare occasions that they *are* described—is 'inert'. In a generous moment, Edmund Wilson defended Snow but anticipated the judgment of history in finding his novels 'almost completely unreadable'. 'The corridors of power' furnished the title for one of Snow's novels; it is all that is left of the work. Things are a little different with 'the two cultures'. The phrase has lived on as a vague popular shorthand for the rift—a matter of incomprehension tinged with hostility—that has grown up between scientists and literary intellectuals in the modern world. Lack of precision has been part of its appeal: to speak of 'the two cultures' is to convey regret, censure, and—since one is bold enough to name and appreciate a presumably unfortunate circumstance—superiority all at once.

Snow first used the famous phrase in 1956 as the title for an article in the *New Statesman*. The article provided the germ for his 1959 Rede Lecture at Cambridge University, 'The Two Cultures and the Scientific Revolution', which was subsequently printed in *Encounter* magazine in two instalments. It is a brief, avuncular work. In book form it fits comfortably into fewer than 60 printed pages and is full of men who 'muck in as colleagues', behaviour that's 'just not on', etc. Yet as soon as it appeared, 'The Two Cultures' became a sensation on both sides of the Atlantic. The edition I have was published in 1961; by then the book was already in its seventh printing.

Its fame got an additional boost a year later when the critic F.R. Leavis published his attack on 'The Two Cultures' in the *Spectator*. Originally delivered as the Downing Lecture at Cambridge, 'Two Cultures? The Significance of C.P.

Snow' is a devastating rhetorical fusillade. It's not just that no two stones of Snow's argument are left standing: each and every pebble is pulverised; the fields are salted; and the entire population is sold into slavery. Leavis spoke of 'the preposterous and menacing absurdity of C.P. Snow's consecrated public standing', heaped derision on his 'embarrassing vulgarity of style', his 'panoptic pseudo-categories', his 'complete ignorance' of history, literature, the history of civilisation, and the human significance of the Industrial Revolution. '[I]t is ridiculous', Leavis wrote, 'to credit him with any capacity for serious thinking about the problems on which he offers to advise the world'. So much for Snow the sage. What about Snow the artist, Snow the novelist? 'Snow is, of course, a—no, I can't say that; he isn't: Snow thinks of himself as a novelist', Leavis thundered, but in fact 'his incapacity as a novelist is … total': 'as a novelist he doesn't exist; he doesn't begin to exist. He can't be said to know what a novel is.' It gets worse. Snow is 'utterly without a glimmer of what creative literature is, or why it matters'. '[N]ot only is he not a genius', Leavis concluded; 'he is intellectually as undistinguished as it is possible to be'.

Literary London was stunned and outraged by Leavis's performance (which was something of an official swan song, since he retired from teaching that year). At that time, a certain degree of rhetorical *politesse* still marked British literary journalism; Leavis had been the opposite of polite. In the weeks that followed, the *Spectator* printed more than 30 irate letters, many from eminent personages, most of them siding firmly with Snow. It was an extraordinary outpouring. One correspondent deplored Leavis's 'insincerity, incapacity and envy'. Lord Boothby, claiming that there was 'not a single constructive thought in his lecture', spoke of Leavis's 'reptilian venom'. Stephen Toulmin wrote that the lecture was 'an insult to the audience and to Snow himself'.

Other indignant commentators dismissed Leavis's lecture as 'ludicrously overdone', 'a demonstration of ill-mannered, self-centered and destructive behaviour', or, more simply, 'bemused drivelling'.

The extreme reaction was partly a response to Leavis's own extremity: Lionel Trilling, reflecting on the controversy in *Commentary*, summed it up when he spoke of the 'unexampled ferocity' and 'bad manners' of Leavis's attack. In fact, Trilling agreed with much that Leavis had to say; but he could not abide the scorched-earth rhetoric: 'it is', he wrote, 'a bad tone, an impermissible tone'. Perhaps so. But in the English response there was also a large element of snobbery: by 1960 Sir Charles was, well, Sir Charles: a member of the Athenaeum, a reviewer for the *New Statesman*, someone whom one *knew*. Thus Dame Edith Sitwell: 'Dr Leavis only attacked Charles because he is famous and writes good English.' *Charles*, indeed.

The ruffled feathers of London's intellectual elite make for an amusing footnote to the cultural history of the period. But the questions raised by 'The Two Cultures'—and by Leavis's searching criticisms of Snow's position—are something more serious. It is not simply that the gulf between scientists and literary intellectuals (and the general public, too, of course) has grown wider as science has become ever more specialised and complex. Because of the extremely technical nature of contemporary scientific discourse—think, for example, of its deep reliance on abstruse mathematical notation—that gulf is unbridgeable and will only widen as knowledge progresses. The more pressing issue concerns the fate of culture in a world increasingly determined by science and technology. Leavis described C.P. Snow as a 'portent' of our civilization because, in his view, Snow's argument epitomised modern society's tendency to trivialise culture by reducing it to a form of diversion or entertainment. Not that diversion and entertainment are necessarily bad things: they have their place; but so do art and high culture. The problem, as Leavis saw, is that the confusion of art and entertainment always proceeds in one direction: toward the adulteration, the trivialisation, of art. For him, it was not surprising that 'The Two Cultures' captured the public imagination: it did so precisely because it pandered to the debased notion of culture championed by established taste.

The year 2000 marked the fortieth anniversary of Snow's essay. As we look around the cultural landscape today, we see the debris of a civilization seemingly bent on cultural suicide: the triumph of pop culture in nearly every sphere of artistic endeavor, the glorification of mindless sensationalism, the attack on the very idea of permanent cultural achievement—in the West, anyway, the final years of the twentieth century were years of unprecedented material wealth coupled with profound cultural and intellectual degradation. C.P. Snow is hardly to blame for all this. He was merely a canary in the mine. But as such—as a symptom, a 'portent'—he still has much to tell us.

Perhaps the first thing that one notices about 'The Two Cultures' is its tone, which vacillates wildly between the cozily anecdotal and the apocalyptic. On the one hand, we find Snow busy meeting the physicist 'W.L. Bragg in the buffet on Kettering station on a very cold morning in 1939'. Without the narrative prop of High Table dinner conversation at Cambridge, Snow would be lost. On the other hand, he insists that the problem he has outlined is a 'problem of the entire West'. 'This is', Snow writes toward the end of his lecture, 'one of the situations where the worst crime is innocence.' In some 'afterthoughts' about the two-cultures controversy that he published in *Encounter* in 1960, Snow refers solemnly to his lecture as a 'call to action'.

But what, exactly, is the problem? And what actions does Snow recommend we take? At one moment it's nothing much; the next it's everything and more. There is that 'gulf of mutual incomprehension' between scientists and 'literary intellectuals', of course. But it soon turns out that there are also the 'three menaces' of nuclear war, overpopulation and the 'gap' between rich and poor nations. (There are many gulfs, gaps, chasms, caesurae in 'The Two Cultures'; it sometimes seems that Snow's entire argument has fallen into one of them.) On one page the problem is reforming the schools so that 'English and American children get a reasonable education'. Well, OK. But a few pages later the problem is mobilising Western resources to industrialise India. And Africa. And Southeast Asia. And Latin America. And the Middle East—all in order to forestall widespread starvation, revolution and anarchy. Snow envisions tens of thousands of engineers from Europe and North America volunteering 'at least ten years out of their lives' to bring the 'scientific revolution' to the underdeveloped parts of the world. Reality check: in Snow's mind, the Soviet Union was way ahead of the West in dealing with these vast imponderables. This is, he says, partly because the Russians have a 'passionate belief in education'. But it is also because they have a 'deeper insight into the scientific revolution than we have, or than the Americans have'. That explains why the world is clamoring for Russian automobiles and airplanes, you see, and also why the Soviets happened to manage their own economy so much more brilliantly than did the West.

If all this seems like a terrible muddle, it is. In truth, there are three sorts of problems in 'The Two Cultures': trivial, non-existent and misunderstood. Some, such as the famous gulf, gap, or chasm between scientists and literary intellectuals, are both trivial and misunderstood. Sure, it would be nice if 'literary intellectuals' knew more science.

But the gulf, gap, chasm that Snow deplores will never be bridged—from this side of the gulf, at any rate—by anyone lacking a good deal of highly specialised training. And, *pace* Snow, it's not at all clear that the gulf really matters.

As several critics have pointed out, Snow's terminology can be exceedingly slippery. He begins with a dichotomy between the world of literary intellectuals and the world of physical scientists. (And he eschews anything more elaborate: 'I have thought a long time about going in for further refinements', Snow writes, 'but in the end I have decided against it': no wonder the biochemist Michael Yudkin, in a perceptive article on 'The Two Cultures', noted that Snow often seems 'more concerned with the number two than the term "culture"'.) But in order to further his gulf-gap-chasm thesis, Snow is soon using 'literary intellectual' interchangeably with 'traditional culture'. This fusion yields the observation that there is 'an unscientific', even an 'anti-scientific' flavour to 'the whole "traditional" culture'. What can this mean? Aristotle, Euclid, Galileo, Copernicus, Descartes, Boyle, Newton, Locke, Kant: are there any more 'traditional' representatives of 'the whole "traditional" culture"'? There's not much anti-scientific aroma emanating from those quarters.[ii] The real burden of Snow's thesis was

---

[ii] Among other things, Snow's lecture illustrates the fact that a mountain of confusion can be built from a grain of truth. For there *is* an ingredient of irrationalism in Western culture that regularly manifests itself in anti-scientific biases of one sort or another. Certain varieties of romanticism belong here, as do many less agreeable phenomena. But Snow, while he dances around this issue—it is what gives his whole 'two cultures' thesis a superficial plausibility—never really comes to terms with it. In contemporary academic culture, a widespread suspicion of the achievements of science—often extending to an outright rejection of the idea of factual truth—can be seen in many radical movements and

accurately summed up by Leavis: 'there are the two uncommunicating and mutually indifferent cultures, there is the need to bring them together, and there is C.P. Snow, whose place in history is that he has them both, so that we have in him the paradigm of the desired and necessary union'.

At the beginning of his lecture, Snow affects a generous even-handedness in his attitude toward scientists and literary intellectuals. There's a bit of criticism for both. If literary types tend to be quite appallingly ignorant of even rudimentary scientific concepts (Snow seems astounded that his writer friends cannot define such basic concepts as mass, acceleration, etc.), then it turns out that many scientists are unacquainted with the novels of Charles Dickens. But this show of even-handedness soon evaporates. The 'culture' of science, Snow tells us, 'contains a great deal of argument, usually much more rigorous, and almost always at a higher conceptual level, than the literary persons' arguments'. Literary intellectuals are 'natural Luddites'; scientists 'have the future in their bones'. This is a formulation that Snow rather likes. 'If the scientists have the future in their bones', he writes later, 'then the traditional culture responds by wishing the future did not exist.' To clinch his argument that

---

'theories'. 'Cultural constructivism', deconstruction, radical feminism, and other fashionable *ists* and *isms* are aggressively anti-empirical. Paul R. Gross and Norman Levitt expertly anatomise these disparate phenomena in *Higher Superstition: The Academic Left and Its Quarrels with Science* (Johns Hopkins, 1994). They show that this new hostility to science is part of a more general hostility to Western values and institutions, an anti-Enlightenment hostility that 'mocks the idea that ... a civilization is capable of progressing from ignorance to insight'.

literary intellectuals (a.k.a. 'the traditional culture') 'wish the future did not exist', Snow holds up ... George Orwell's *Nineteen Eighty-four*—as if that harrowing admonitory tale could have been written by anyone who did not have a passionate concern for the future!

Snow is especially impatient with what he takes to be the politics of 'the traditional culture'. He quotes approvingly an unnamed 'scientist of distinction' who opined that literary intellectual writers tended to be 'not only politically silly, but politically wicked. Didn't the influence of all they represent bring Auschwitz that much closer?' In this context, Snow explicitly mentions Yeats, Wyndham Lewis and Ezra Pound. But his indictment is actually much broader: 'nine-tenths' of the great literary figures of the early twentieth century (he specifies the period 1914-1950) are on his reckoning politically suspect. The 'culture' of science, on the contrary, is optimistically forward-looking. But not, Snow hastens to add, *shallowly* optimistic. Scientists, too, appreciate the tragic nature of human life—that each of us 'dies alone'. But they are wise enough to distinguish, with Snow, between the 'individual condition and the social condition' of man. There is, Snow writes, 'no reason why, just because the individual condition is tragic, so must the social condition be'. The prospect of social improvement (what Snow, echoing a character from *Alice in Wonderland*, picturesquely calls the prospect of 'jam tomorrow') is a galvanising force that allows the individual to transcend, or at least to forget, his private destiny.

Snow's argument operates by erasing or ignoring certain fundamental distinctions. He goes to a literary party, discovers that no one (except himself) can explain the second law of thermodynamics, and then concludes triumphantly: 'yet I was asking something which is about the equivalent of *Have you read a work of Shakespeare's?'* But, as Leavis notes, 'there *is* no scientific equivalent of that question; equations between orders so disparate are meaningless'. The second law of thermodynamics is a piece of specialised knowledge, useful or irrelevant depending on the job to be done; the works of Shakespeare provide a window into the soul of humanity: to read them is tantamount to acquiring self-knowledge. Snow seems blind to this distinction.[iii] A similar confusion is at work in Snow's effort to neutralise individuality by assimilating it to the project of 'social hope'. That may sound nobly altruistic. But, as Leavis asks, 'What *is* the "social condition" that has nothing to do with the "individual condition"?'

> What is the 'social hope' that transcends, cancels or makes indifferent the inescapable tragic condition of each individual? Where, if not in individuals, is what is hoped for ... to be located? Or are we to find the reality of life in hoping for other people a kind of felicity about which as proposed for ourselves ('jam', Snow calls it later—we die alone, but there's jam to be had first) we have no illusions?

Leavis here exposes the central philistinism, the deeply *anti*-cultural bias, of Snow's position: the idea that the individual is merely a fungible token, a representative type, whose ultimate value is purely a function of his place in the tapestry of society.

In the end, Snow is a naïve meliorist. For him, a society's material standard of living provides the ultimate, really the only, criterion of 'the good life'; science is the means of

---

[iii] Curiously, he also seems oblivious of the extent to which the second law of thermodynamics has impressed itself—vividly if not always accurately—upon the imaginations of modern artists, philosophers, and theologians via the concept of entropy: the thought that the universe is ineluctably 'winding down' has proven to be a deeply unsettling but also fertile metaphor.

raising the standard of living, ergo science is the arbiter of value. Culture—literary, artistic culture—is merely a patina or gloss added to the substance of material wealth to make it shine more brightly. It provides us with no moral challenge or insight, because the only serious questions are how to keep increasing and effectively distributing the world's wealth, and these are not questions culture is competent to address. 'The upshot' of Snow's argument, Leavis writes, 'is that if you insist on the need for any other kind of concern, entailing forethought, action and provision, about the human future—any other kind of misgiving—than that which talks in terms of productivity, material standards of living, hygienic and technological progress, then you are a Luddite.'

It is worth pausing at this point to note that Leavis grants Snow's subsidiary argument that improvements in scientific education would be a good thing. Leavis is not 'anti-scientific'. *Of course* 'standards of living, hygienic and technological progress' are important. None of that is at issue. Nor is Leavis in any way suggesting that one should 'defy, or try to reverse, the accelerating movement of external civilisation ... that is determined by advancing technology'. Barring a world-extinguishing catastrophe, the progress of science is inexorable. Leavis accepts that. What he denies is that science is a *moral* resource—he denies, that is to say, that there is any such thing as a 'culture' of science. Science tells us how best to do things we have already decided to do, not why we should do them. Its province is the province of *means* not *ends*. That is its glory—and its limitation.

This is something that the editors of the *Spectator* grasped much more clearly than the many correspondents who wrote in to complain about Leavis's essay. One word that is missing from Snow's essay, they note in an unsigned editorial, is 'philosophy'—'that effort to impart moral direction that was found in the best nineteenth-century English writers'. Chief among 'the best nineteenth-century English writers' was Leavis's own model and inspiration, Matthew Arnold. It is one of history's small but delicious coincidences that in 1882, nearly 80 years before C.P. Snow's Rede Lecture, Arnold was chosen for that honour. His Rede Lecture—'Literature and Science'—was itself a kind of 'two cultures' argument. But his point was essentially the opposite of Snow's. Written in response to T.H. Huxley's insistence that literature should and inevitably would be supplanted by science, Arnold argued that, 'so long as human nature is what it is', culture would continue to provide mankind with its fulcrum of moral understanding.

The *tenor* of Arnold's lecture could not have been more different from Leavis's. 'The tone of tentative inquiry, which befits a being of dim faculties and bounded knowledge, is the tone I would wish to take', Arnold noted with un-Leavisite modesty. But his argument anticipated Leavis in striking detail. Both are concerned with what Leavis called 'the cultural consequences of the technological revolution'. Both argued passionately against the trivialisation of culture, against what Arnold dismissed as 'a superficial humanism' that is 'mainly decorative'. And both looked to culture to provide a way of relating, in Arnold's words, the 'results of modern science' to 'our need for conduct, our need for beauty'. This is the crux: that culture is in some deep sense inseparable from *conduct*—from that unscientific but ineluctable question, 'How should I live my life?' Leavis's point was the same. The stunning upheavals precipitated by the march of science and technology had rendered culture—the arts and humanities—both more precarious and more precious. Leavis understood that the preservation of culture —not as entertainment or diversion but as a guide to 'conduct' — was now more crucial than ever. If mankind was to confront the moral challenges of modern science 'in full intelligent possession of its humanity' and maintain 'a basic living deference towards that to which, opening as it does into the unknown and itself unmeasurable, we know we belong', then the realm of culture had to be protected from the reductive forces of a crude scientific rationalism.

The contemporary relevance of this argument can hardly be overestimated. We live at a moment when 'the results of science' confront us daily with the most extreme moral challenges. Abortion on demand, nanotechnology, the prospect of genetic engineering — the list is long and sobering. But more challenging that any particular application of science is the widespread assumption that *every* problem facing mankind is susceptible to technological intervention and control. In this situation, the temptation to reduce culture to a reservoir of titillating pastimes is all but irresistible. Rock music, 'performance art', television, video games (not to mention drugs, violence, and promiscuous sex): we are everywhere encouraged to think of ourselves as complicated machines for consuming sensations — the more, and more exotic, the better. Culture is no longer an invitation to confront our humanity but a series of opportunities to impoverish it through diversion. We are, as Eliot put it in *Four Quartets*, 'distracted from distraction by distraction'. C.P. Snow represents the smiling, jovial face of this predicament. Critics like Arnold and Leavis offer us the beginnings of an alternative. Many people objected to the virulence of Leavis's attack on Snow. But given the din of competing voices, it is a wonder that he was heard at all.

The Eunuch at the Orgy: Reflections on the Significance of F.R. Leavis[(i)]

Raymond Tallis

It is nearly 30 years since F.R. Leavis, infuriated by the wide currency given to the views advanced in Snow's Rede Lecture,[1] responded with a lecture of his own. As was widely observed at the time, the Richmond Lecture 'The Significance of C.P. Snow'[2] plumbed new depths in academic debate. Instead of attacking Snow's arguments, Leavis attacked Snow; for he saw Snow's lecture not as containing a case to be answered but as itself a portent of a degenerate culture. In a prose almost crippled by the weight of sarcastic intent, he asserted that Snow — whose status as a 'Sage' infuriated him — had an 'undistinguished mind', apparently about as undistinguished as it was possible to possess this side of coma. He supported this assertion not by demonstrating faults in Snow's arguments but by spiteful reference to the latter's novels. He stopped just short of saying that Snow had an ugly face and that he served damned filthy sherry.

Even at this distance, Leavis's sneers have the power to shock, to anger and to disgust. The immediate result of his lecture was that the question of 'The Two Cultures' ceased to be a subject of serious debate and became instead a delicious scandal. The long-term result is that the deplorable situation to which Snow had drawn attention, in an admittedly crass, at times vulgar and somewhat self-regarding fashion, has

---

[(i)] First published as Chapter 3 of *Newton's Sleep: Two Cultures and Two Kingdoms*, London: Macmillan, 1995.

not altered in the slightest. The 'omnescience' described earlier demonstrates how, as we approach the twenty-first century,[ii] many of those trained in the humanities have yet to catch up with the science of the sixteenth.

There is little point in rehearsing Snow's case; the facts about the omnescience of humanist intellectuals that he deplored cannot be denied and things have not improved since he wrote. There is equally little purpose in combing Leavis's response for reasoned dissent: there is none. So why blow on the embers of an old dispute that Leavis reduced to an undignified squabble? Why tilt at windbags? Precisely because Leavis's anger and his refusal of argument are symptomatic, and his attitude towards science is still widespread among those who teach or who have been trained in the humanities. Even those who diverge from his political, literary-critical and pedagogic views acknowledge his importance as the individual who placed 'English Studies' at the heart of humanities teaching in the universities, and as 'undoubtedly the single most influential figure in twentieth-century English literary criticism'.[3] This influence is transmitted not only by his writings and the writings of those who have been influenced by him but also, and perhaps more importantly, through the example of his personality and his posturing. The embattled visionary, surrounded by ignorant, corrupt and unredeemably narrow

[ii] In the opening chapter of the book, first published in 1995, from which this essay is taken 'omnescience' (*not* omniscience) is the term used to describe the attitude of 'humanist intellectuals who, ignorant of science themselves, have been influential in ensuring that such ignorance should be acceptable and that a knowledge and understanding of science should not be regarded as central to general education'. Tallis, R., *Newton's Sleep: Two Cultures and Two Kingdoms*, London: Macmillan, 1995, p. 3.

and stupid (or shallowly clever) adversaries, the profound thinker at odds with a frivolous and superficial age, an age consumed by greed and, because it has lost touch with the deeper realities of nature and human feelings, devoid of true values, is an attractive role model—even for those who would repudiate Leavis himself. Internalising such a role model as one's self-image makes it possible to live an unhurried existence within the walls of an institute of higher learning, adding to the ant-heap of exegesis under which canonical but unread works are buried, and still enjoy a sense of permanent moral superiority, rather than recognise oneself as a high-consuming mouth making a contribution of uncertain value to the productive process.[4]

The vulnerability of Leavis's central positions, insofar as they can be discerned through the fog of rage and self-righteousness, has often been noted. Raymond Williams's critique of the mythical 'organic community' that Leavis used as a stick to beat the modern world was definitive. As he pointed out in *Culture and Society*,[5] Leavis overlooks the exploitation and penury that dominated pre-industrial rural life. Williams refrained from observing that there is something particularly hypocritical about a man, whose means of subsistence comes from writing words about words, books about books, advocating for others a life marked by more direct contact with nature. Leavis's habit of existential self-refutation is equally impressive in his assumption of the Arnoldian mantle while laying down the law in a decidedly non-Arnoldian manner. Arnold's rejection of provinciality, and his emphasis on the need 'to get yourself out of the way' so that you can 'see the object as it really is', were mocked in Leavis's own example.

So Leavis is an important indicator of the level of confusion at which one is permitted to operate in certain 'disciplines' while still commanding a hearing. He is, in this crucial sense, a representative figure. To use a Leavisite formula, Leavis exhibits 'a multiple typicality'; and to see this is to be reminded of how alien the standards of discussion routine in science are to many trained in the humanities. And to see also, perhaps, why to them science seems so remote that ignorance of it hardly counts as ignorance at all. Leavis would rank high in the demonology of an intellectual culture that valued rigour and the search for truth. Instead, he is 'the most influential figure in twentieth-century English literary criticism'. Nothing could be further from the scientist contributing to a collaborative international research effort, building with others and on the work of many thousands of others, than this solitary know-all articulating his tastes as if they were revealed truths.

Even more pertinent to our present argument is what Leavis actually retained from Arnold. In his charitable assessment of the Leavis/Snow controversy,[6] Lionel Trilling, in a manner reminiscent of a parent dealing with an angry and upset child, tries to work out 'what the matter is': Snow's unpardonable crime is apparently that he does not agree with Leavis's quasi-Arnoldian position that literature (and only literature) is 'criticism of life'. For Trilling this is an explanation, even a vindication, of Leavis's response, though it does not excuse his venomously bad manners. What Trilling's explanation lets slip is the assumption, widespread among non-scientists, that science is not also a criticism of life—and at the deepest level. It is assumed that science is part of the life that has to be criticised by the educated, part of the object that the educated mind may inspect (from a great distance), and not part of the mind itself or crucial to its education. This was not precisely the position that Arnold himself held (in a considerably more polite exchange) against Huxley—as we shall discuss presently. The assumption that science is not criticism of life is, of course, untenable. From Copernicus onwards, the findings and speculations of the scientists have been a continuous threat to collective, unreflective beliefs about the nature and purpose of human life, the position of man in the order of things and the origin and destination of the universe; in short 'a criticism of life' in the best and deepest sense.

Trilling's charitable diagnosis of the Richmond tantrum also overlooks the extent to which it was a reflex response to a perceived threat: Snow's views undermined Leavis's sense of his own position in the scheme of things. Leavis was not alone in experiencing that threat but his response is most revealing. The anger behind the Richmond Lecture is the anger of an all-knowing man encountering the suggestion that his knowledge is severely limited and that what he knows may not be as central as he had thought. To realise that there are more things in heaven and earth than are dreamt of in the curricula of departments of English is, for someone like Leavis, unbearable anguish that must be avoided at all costs.

This is betrayed in the last few pages of the Richmond Lecture where he suddenly becomes coherent. Like Snow, he says he looks to the university to be 'a centre of human consciousness: perception, knowledge, judgement and responsibility'. Unlike Snow, however, he would see 'the centre of such a university *in a vital English School*' [emphasis added]—which would consequently be the centre of a centre of human consciousness. The megalomaniacal claims for such a school—concentrating on training for maturity in literary studies—have been characterised by Norris in his introduction to *F.R. Leavis*: the school would 'be the one hope of renewal and growth in an otherwise irredeemable "mass-civilisation"'.[7]

One catches a glimpse of such fantasies in Leavis's reference, towards the end of his Richmond Lecture, to the 'essential Cambridge' that he holds up against the 'academic Cambridge' he associates with Snow. The 'essential Cambridge' turns out to be Dr and Mrs Leavis and a few like-minded friends. A comparison with the non-essential Cambridge is instructive. In the decades in which Leavis was at Downing, the non-essential Cambridge was transforming our conception of the nature of matter, laying the foundations of the new astrophysics, creating whole new branches of mathematics, and, in the legendary Medical Research Council laboratory, making some of the most important discoveries in the entire 2,000-year history of biology. These included working out the structure of DNA — and so advancing our understanding of genetics and of cell biology. This eventually made possible many developments which before had not been dreamt of: gene therapy for congenital diseases, transgenic species to increase food production in places where starvation is the condition of daily life, a deeper understanding of the mechanisms of carcinogenesis. These discoveries, aside from their practical significance, also had the capability of transforming our sense of our nature. For Leavis, apparently, this was small beer compared with the work of the essential Cambridge: proving to its own satisfaction that Charlotte Yonge was an important forgotten novelist; that Dickens was childish, uneducated and immature; that Richard Jeffreys was probably superior to Thomas Hardy; that Dickens did, after all, write one 'completely serious work of art'; that Flaubert, Proust and others were not worth reading; that Dickens was the Shakespeare of the novel, etc. (All the different views on Dickens were published by Leavis at one time or another. They are documented in Michael Bell's book on Leavis.)

Leavis's claims can be understood as a response to deep anxiety. For what the 'essential' Cambridge must have found difficult to accept—because it undermined its own claim to centrality—was that, for good or ill, the major intellectual and social event of recent centuries had been the progress of science, and the transformation of our world and world picture this brought about. This anxiety, and the denial it gives rise to, is widespread in the humanities. This is not surprising; for it cannot be pleasant for the innumerate to discover the centrality of the mathematisation of nature to our culture; or for those whose professional business is ultimately with matters of taste to be reminded of the importance of the unattainably different level of rigour and conceptual sophistication prevailing in subjects of which they have little understanding. Auden spoke of feeling when amongst scientists like 'a shabby curate among bishops'.

It is easier for those like Auden whose literary achievements are undoubted than for those who work as literary critics to admit to such feelings. And the uneasiness may cut much deeper. One thinks of the eunuch at the orgy who has always been first with the gossip and knows who does what to and with whom. One day, he is forced to realise that he doesn't really know what is going on. Unable to experience sexual desire himself, he realises that his knowledge is not real knowledge. Far from being the centre of things, he is forever on the margin.

More sophisticated defensive reactions are available to those for whom the most important fact about science is that it marginalises their own activities. One is to assert that science is essentially dehumanising, as Bryan Appleyard[8] has asserted, and to suggest that the industrialisation of death in modern wars is an expression not only of the technological possibilities opened up by science but also of the spirit of science itself; that we should see the concentration camp, rather than the washing machine, antibiotics or international airlifts of food aid, as typical consequences of the application of the scientific method. The implication is that the less we know about science the better it will be for our humanity.

Another way of reasserting the centrality of literary studies to human consciousness and so of marginalising scientific knowledge—so that to be ignorant of science is not to be importantly ignorant—is to offset lack of true knowledge by increased knowingness. This is like the eunuch compensating for never having experienced the sexual desire that makes inner sense of the outwardly senseless behaviour of the others at the orgy simply by knowing much more of the gossip than anyone else. He is uniquely expert on everyone else's amatory gyrations. This compensatory increase in knowingness is reflected in developments in the field of literary studies.

I have elsewhere discussed (*Not Saussure* and *In Defence of Realism*) the displacement of literary criticism by literary theory and the expansion of the scope of literary theory to encompass all discourses, not merely literary ones. Theorists are able to 'place' texts, in the sense of putting them in their place. This has been most widely touted as a strategy to deal with the sense of inferiority a literary critic may feel towards creative artists (see *In Defence of Realism*); but it also serves to deal with Auden's 'shabby curate' syndrome. The theorist, who floats above all texts, is not marginalised by any of them. He can forget that he has not the faintest inkling of the techniques of science, that he could not follow most scientific papers beyond the first paragraph, that the mathematical methods and the statistical techniques which are the true heart of science are unknown to him.

A particular example of this strategy is 'narrative theory' which treats science, philosophy, literature and literary criticism etc. simply as different modes of story-telling. Cristopher Nash's *Narrative in Culture* collection[9] exemplifies this approach. Rom Harré's contribution, 'Some Conventions of Scientific Discourse', is especially pertinent.

Harré argues that scientific documents 'are far from unvarnished descriptions of uncontested facts'. Scientific discourse has adopted 'a peculiar rhetoric' of 'deindexicalisation' (in which, for example, the third person is preferred over the first person singular) in order to give the impression of objective truth. But what is presented as 'the' truth is merely the truth according to a certain community whose membership is closely regulated. One of the modes of entry to the scientific community is to learn to get difficult equipment working; one knows one has got such equipment working when one gets the results the community approves of. There is a circle of mutual legitimation here—a circle that is closed off against any genuine access to nature itself. In addition, character references may support one's claims to being one of what Harré calls the 'good guys': 'personal character is often quoted as an epistemic warrant'.

The aim of Harré's 'microsociology of scientists' is obviously to debunk science. Those who wish to cut science down to size, and so to rationalise their own ignorance of it, may try to relativise its truths, as Harré does, by 'demonstrating' on the basis of anecdotes, gossip etc. that science consists of tales that command respect primarily because they have been accredited by a certain group of cognoscenti. And this will be very gratifying to those who may be oppressed by the comparative lack of rigour of their own subjects. Scientists, like literary critics, are in the business of getting their stories ('HIV is the cause of AIDS', 'Dickens is a childish, immature novelist') believed.

Harré's own story carries a momentary plausibility—and has transient appeal to someone like me who always has trouble getting his apparatus to work—but this passes as soon as one reflects on the fact that the activity he is describing as simply another exercise in story-telling has utterly transformed man's sense of himself, his power of acting on the world, and the form and content of his daily life. Our whole lives are embedded in the embodiments of the practical truths of science. And the speed with which this has come about is astounding. As John Maynard Smith[10] has pointed out, if a two-hour film were made of vertebrate evolution, tool-making man would appear in the last minute; and the period between the invention of the steam engine and the use of nuclear power would take less than a hundredth of a second. And to take a specific example of the utmost contemporary importance: the recognition of AIDS as a specific disease, the establishment of its cause, the precise delineation of the extraordinarily complex effects of the virus, the beginnings of a strategy for searching for a cure, have all been accomplished in little more than a decade. At the beginning of the 1980s, the terrible spectacle of young men deliquescing to pus before their horrified doctors' eyes was utterly mysterious; now the causative agent has been identified and it is better known than any other plant or animal virus. The idea, so obvious now, that the procession of rare diseases suffered by certain homosexual men in New York was the manifestation of immune deficiency, that this could be brought about by a virus, and that the virus did this by writing itself into DNA (reverse transcription) is a series of daring leaps of understanding, all the more daring for being constrained by the discipline of a careful and complex science.

None of this seems to puzzle Harré or make him question his 'rhetorical analysis'. Alan Gross's critique of the truth claims of the natural sciences is even more deeply rooted in a rhetorical analysis of scientific discourse. Style in science, he claims:

> is not a window on reality, but the vehicle of an ideology that systematically misdescribes experimental and observational events. It is their ideological stance that makes contemporary scientists the legitimate heirs of medieval theologians: theirs is not a dispassionate search for truth, but a passionate conviction that the truth is their quotidian business.[11]

Science has no privileged access to the truth about the natural world: its special authority is socially constructed and it has rhetorical force but no ontological or epistemological basis: 'science is less a matter of truth than of making words' and science has no special relationship to nature: it is simply the sum of all the things the scientific community can, by fair means or foul, persuade itself to believe. Scientific knowledge is not special but social, the result not of discovery of what is out there but of persuasion as to what is out there.

He illustrates the rule of rhetoric in scientific discourse by a detailed analysis of the famous understatement at the end of Crick and Watson's paper of 1953 describing the structure of DNA: 'It has not escaped our notice that the specific pairing mechanism we have postulated immediately suggests a possible copying mechanism for the genetic material'. The rhetorical figures here are irony and understatement. He could not have chosen an example more damaging to his own case. The Crick and Watson paper lies at the head of 40 years of molecular biology. The helical structure of DNA has been confirmed as objective fact repeatedly since then and it has led to a myriad of other major discoveries that have profoundly changed our approach to, for example, the diagnosis and treatment of disease. The use of gene therapy to treat otherwise untreatable diseases, a direct result of insights based upon the Crick and Watson paper, has proved that scientific discoveries are not mere rhetoric. Gross may believe that scientists are susceptible to rhetoric but he cannot, surely, believe that cells are.

If science were merely the art of persuasion, the deployment of rhetorical tropes and the mobilisation of social forces, in order to impose a view of the world upon others, then it is impossible to see how science could have ever been effective. Why does this word processor work, why do antibiotics cure, why do plane navigation systems guide people across the world, if the underlying science has no relationship to natural reality but is merely the result of a shouting match in which the most charismatic figures and the most cunning arguers are able to carry the day? As Feynman famously said at the end of his personal report on the NASA disaster: 'For a successful technology, reality must take precedence over public relations, for nature cannot be fooled.'[12] Non-human matter, over which science has given human beings such enormous power, is not impressed by rhetoric. Likewise, if science really were as Rom Harré (who is himself deeply knowledgeable about science) portrays it in 'Some Conventions of Scientific Discourse'—a social activity in which truth is established at least in part by the authority and charisma of the high priests and by the activities of acolytes who secure admission to the priesthood by getting their apparatus to work—we should have scarcely moved out of the Stone Age.[13] Every hi-tech regulator of our environment that works reliably, every successful treatment of overwhelming infection, every word processor that enacts its routine miracles of information processing, is a testament to an objective truth in science that may not be absolute (whatever that may mean) but which goes far beyond the kind of clique-consensus truths that Harré and Gross focus on.

Rhetoric and social forces of course play a part in the collective enterprise of science, just as they do in other human activities. But they are not the only factors; indeed, they are less important here than in every other human activity. The accumulated heritage of Western science—all that distances us from Thales and Pythagoras—is precisely what goes beyond rhetoric and herd behaviour; the things that survive the fading of the rhetoric in the journal and the lecture hall and the changing of the herd. Harré's and Gross's account of science does not distinguish between science and Lysenko-science. Of course the bullshitters and the liars may hold front-stage for a while. But in the end they are found out and their 'contributions' (unlike those of Ampere, Maxwell, Boltzmann, Crick, *et al.*) are forgotten. Time weeds out the few results that are established on the basis of the charisma of charlatans. Nor does it explain why science-based technology is powerful and magic impotent.

Others within the humanities have taken heart from trends in the philosophy of science which they read as suggesting that scientific theories, formulated within certain paradigms (to use Thomas Kuhn's phrase), are like so many fashions that replace one another for external rather than internal reasons. The power of the Kuhnian critique of science[14] has been exaggerated: the relativising simplifications it has been reduced to cannot take account of the success of science and the fact that it indubitably progresses. Einstein's theories did not invalidate Newton's contribution; on the contrary, they defined more precisely the scope of the Newtonian world picture. Newton's mechanics is not false, except in its assumption of universality: it is true for a world in which the speed of light is infinite and sufficient for most of everyday life where motions are considered whose velocity is small compared with that of the speed of light. The mathematical techniques discovered by the Greeks are the foundations of modern mathematical physics. Copernican astronomy built on Ptolemaic. Much of what Archimedes discovered still stands 2,500 years later. Recent advances have not discredited or disproved Harvey's discovery of the circulation of the blood, Hamilton's method of analysing motion, Clerk Maxwell's prediction of radio waves etc.

We tend to exaggerate the errors of the past and the extent to which the science of one generation differs from those of preceding generations precisely because enduring theories that are not overthrown by subsequent discoveries become assimilated into the general scientific world picture; they become part of the ground upon which contemporary science stands. Unsuccessful theories of the past are more visible for this reason than successful ones.

In short, the rate at which hypotheses are born and die in the privacy of scientists' minds and in the publicity of the scientific journals does not prove the relativity of scientific truth: the strong hypotheses overthrown have contributed to the growth of science by stimulating experiment and focusing thought. In many cases—as with Einstein's 'overthrow' of Newtonian thought—the theories of the past are not so much proven false as demonstrated to have limited application. So there is a gradual accumulation of truth; or truth is approached by successive approximations. There is a common pool of ideas and applications growing from all directions.

The Harré and Gross approach to the philosophy and history of science, and to the evaluation of the achievements of scientists, is one that has, in recent years, become distressingly familiar. It is the latest manifestation of the programme of the Sociology of Knowledge adumbrated many years ago by Karl Mannheim. Wolpert[15] has lucidly and succinctly surveyed the present scene in his devastating critique of the Strong Programme of the Sociology of Scientific Knowledge (SSK). The SSK programme advocates abandoning the idea of science 'as a privileged or even separate domain of activity and enquiry'. Science must be understood not as a means of acquiring objective general truths about the world but as simply another form of social behaviour. Scientific laws are the product of consensus—and must be understood in terms of the prejudices, social pressures and power relations that result in the emergence of consensus and not in terms of advances in understanding, in logical consistency or correspondence with external reality. In this respect it is no different from any other form of knowledge.

The trouble with this 'rampant relativism' (to use Wolpert's term) is that it undermines itself: the claim of SSK's proponents to have acquired objective knowledge about science must itself be simply a matter of rhetoric, socially conditioned and culturally determined. This problem is additional to the failure of SSK to explain the extraordinary success of science in enhancing our power to control the natural world or to predict its behaviour—to explain why, if scientific discourse has nothing to do with natural reality, streptomycin does and magic does not cure TB. Is this a question of the mycobacterium being less frightened by the group dynamics of priests than of those of microbiologists? By focusing on secondary issues—the means by which scientific reputations are established, the motivation behind research, the prejudices of scientists— SSK proponents manage to distract from the central astonishing fact: the incredible scope and power of scientific approaches and scientific thought that are quite unlike anything else in human life.[16]

The irony is that the image of science projected by the proponents of SSK is a more accurate portrait of their own practices than of the practices of physicists and biologists. In the absence of external tests (including the stringent tests that scientific theories endure in the real world of application: is the disease cured, does the space rocket get to the moon, does the bridge stand up, does the word processor store or destroy data?), theses can become established only by an emergent consensus to be carried by rhetoric and the persuasiveness of charismatic individuals. Without the discipline of 'Is it true?', backed up by the harsher discipline of 'Does it work?', there is only rhetoric. SSK is nearer to the world of literary critics—the world of F.R. Leavis and unargued assertions backed up by the assumption of moral superiority and scorn ('*The Ambassadors* is a work of Henry James's senility')—than to the world of real science. It is precisely when one is in the realm of the untestable that rhetoric, personal power, *argumentum ad hominem*, refutation or support by *argumentum ad situationem* come to the fore. Lenard's dismissal of relativity as 'Jewish physics' or Lysenko's successful advocacy of Lamarckian genetics because it was politically correct are the exceptions in science; outside of science, they are, alas, the rule.

Other debunkers of science focus on science fraud. Fraud certainly occurs in science; there have been celebrated instances. But such instances are few enough to be celebrated. Let us suppose that science fraud has been under-estimated. Let us make a wild accusation and suggest that, instead of the handful of papers out of the millions that are published, five per cent are fraudulent; this would still make science uniquely honest among human activities. Science fraud attracts so much attention *because* it is comparatively rare. Outside of science, one would be grateful if five per cent of documents were *not* fraudulent. If only as few as five per cent of discourses in politics were fraudulent! Scientific papers are subjected to a rigorous process of usually anonymous peer review. The universal human inclination to deceit is less easily gratified in science and brings fewer, less certain and shorter-lasting rewards there than elsewhere. Outside of the exact sciences, much of what passes for disciplined discourse is such that tests of verifiability or predictive value cannot be applied. It would be difficult to imagine testing any of Leavis's self-contradictory, but authoritative, pronouncements on Dickens for truth or accuracy. There the question of fraud can hardly arise because there is no truth to be fabricated, only positions to be advanced.

Of course scientific rigour cannot be extended to all areas of human life and there are legitimate fields of enquiry and scholarship where the scientific method is inappropriate. Nevertheless, those whose experience of disciplined thought has been confined to the humanities (or the innumeracies), where opinion often reigns supreme over ascertainable fact and testable laws are unheard of, cannot be considered as adequately educated. There will be many aspects of contemporary life—from the interpretation of opinion polls to environmental issues—they will not be able to think about intelligently. A scholar who can discriminate the six modes of sensibility in Saint-Amant but has not yet caught up with Copernicus should not rationalise his ignorance but amend it; otherwise he will be as much a plaything of politicians in relation to the major issues of our time as the readers of the more downmarket tabloids.

Re-reading C.P. Snow and His Elusive Search for Authority

Frank Furedi

There were good reasons why C.P. Snow's 'The Two Cultures' resonated with the temper of the times. His 1959 lecture spoke to a growing mood of unease with Western society's cultural and intellectual inheritance. Economic and technological change appeared to call into question the traditions that still influenced the key institutions of public life. Britain's cultural elites felt estranged from the very institutions into which they were socialised. There was a growing consensus that Britain's traditional values and institutions were suffocating society. This was the time when the invective of the Angry Young Men—a loose collections of playwrights and writers—towards 'outdated' class hierarchy gained a widespread hearing. The response of the Establishment was to distance itself from its past and to look for an alternative source of authority. Technology and the harnessing of science to the project of modernisation was self-consciously embraced by many as a solution to the crisis of traditional authority. By the time C.P. Snow delivered his lecture British society was more than ready for his forceful and passionate affirmation for the project of modernisation as well as his scathing attack on traditional authority.

The appeal of Snow's exhortation to modernise was not confined to Britain. The kind of self-doubt that afflicted the British Establishment was also evident, albeit in a more muted form, in other Western societies. The launching of Sputnik 1 by the Soviet Union two years before Snow's lecture provoked a major crisis of confidence in the West about its capacity successfully to adapt to rapidly changing and challenging circumstances. The clearest symptom of this crisis of confidence was the defensive tone with which Western governments and intellectuals responded to this event. Some went so far as to argue that the Soviet Union possessed the kind of formidable potential for innovation and dynamism that the West could not match. In the United States leading commentators declared that the Soviet Union 'had found ways to mobilise the intellectual and economic capacities of its citizens while Americans frittered away their patrimony in mindless consumption and frivolous amusements'.[1] As is often the case in times of unease, anxiety about society's capacity to adapt was focused on the institution of education. It was widely believed that the Soviet Union's educational system was 'superior to our own in its ability to motivate youngsters and enlist them in the nation's enterprises'.[2] So when Snow concluded his lecture with the warning that they had to look at 'education with fresh eyes' and that there was a 'good deal to learn from the Russians' his audience would have known what he was talking about.[3]

On one level 'The Two Cultures' thesis can be interpreted as an exploration of the damaging consequences of the inability of the humanities and science to communicate with one another. His conceptualisation of a split between two intellectual cultures and his critique of the excessive specialisation of the British education system raised interesting questions about what it means to be an educated person. Indeed today, when there is almost no communication across the disciplines and when the intellectual fragmentation of academic life has acquired a pathological character, it is instructive to reflect on the issues raised by Snow. However, when re-reading the lecture one is struck by the impression that Snow has little to say about how to forge an intellectual culture that can draw on contributions from all fields of knowledge and even less to indicate how education can advance such a dialogue. The principal concern of his lecture is to call into question the legacy of the past and gain support for the project of modernisation.

If Snow were alive today he would find it difficult to complain about the hegemony of literary intellectuals basking in the glory of traditional culture. There are very few people inhabiting contemporary Britain who would fit his description of those who 'still like to pretend that traditional culture is the whole of "culture"'.[4] Arguably such people were already becoming culturally marginalised in the late fifties. Today in the twenty-first century the very term 'traditional culture' has the connotation of a historical curiosity with little relevance for people's lives. When used as an adjective—traditional morality, traditional family, traditional authority, traditional values—the word conveys the sense of being outdated and irrelevant. In the sphere of education, traditional teaching methods are equated with bad practice and contemporary pedagogy is wedded to the idea of constantly modernising the curriculum.

However, the decline of the literary intellectual has not been paralleled by the rise in the cultural valuation of science. Although science plays a central role in the development of twenty-first century society, its authority is continually questioned by powerful anti-scientific cultural currents.[5] C.P. Snow, who had a modernist attachment to the achievement of economic growth through scientific innovation, would be disappointed by the erosion of belief in this perspective. He would certainly be shocked by the lack of interest in science by schoolchildren and by its decline as an academic subject. Numerous bureaucratic projects promoting 'the public understanding of science' serve as testimony to the erosion of the modernist enthusiasm it enjoyed in the post-war years. It is far from evident what he would make of circumstances where the devaluation of traditional culture coexists with the loss of cultural authority of science.

The modernising imperative that inspired Snow's outlook has lost much of its force during the past 50 years. Scientific advance and technological innovation continues to improve the quality of life in Western society. But the status of science-led modernisation exists in an ambiguous relationship with powerful anti-modernist sentiments that adopt a pessimistic evaluation of technological innovation and economic growth. In hindsight it appears that 'The Two Cultures' expressed the aspirations of an era that would soon come to an end. By the late sixties modernity itself would be challenged by cultural movements that were becoming alienated from and increasingly hostile to technocracy and modernisation. Disappointment with the promise of science coexisted with the rise of anti-rational trends that questioned the status of Truth in either its traditional or Enlightenment form.[6] Both of the cultures described by Snow had their share of the problems.

It is worth noting that both sides of the cultural divide discussed by Snow were in significant respects the products of the Enlightenment. The Enlightenment furnished scientific knowledge with unprecedented authority and status. Scientific knowledge was embraced by Western societies as the foundation for the construction of a civilized and prosperous life. Of course the role of science was always contested, not least by those who felt that it threatened traditional authority. Traditionalism, the self-conscious affirmation of values and institutions that were once regarded as beyond question, represented a counterpoint to the modernist imagination. But it too was the product of the cultural currents that encouraged the ascendancy of scientific authority. The debate between science and tradition was influenced by political and economic calculations but it was also an intellectually productive discussion about the meaning and content of life and education. In this debate both the humanities and science took themselves seriously and the discussion was not whether or not to value intellectual life but what should be its meaning. Today, questions about the role of the sciences and of the humanities in education seldom acquire the form of a debate about substance. Increasingly, concerns about the intellectual content of education have given way to narrow technical ones about the organisation of the curriculum.

The old debate about the role of the humanities and of the sciences in education has given way to arguments about whether traditional academic subjects as such should be taught at all. As I write the publication of an interim review of the primary curriculum for England proposes to get rid of traditional subjects in favour of cross-curricula teaching.[7] Another advocate of an 'aims-led' rather than a subject-focused curriculum has casually dismissed academic-discipline-based teaching with the words 'discrete subjects are not the only ways of generating intellectual pleasure—if they do at all, that is'.[8] Confusion about what constitutes the overall intellectual vision inspiring education means that neither humanities nor the sciences exercise a dominant influence over education. So what would Snow have made of the fate of the two cultures today?

The problem of adaptation

Outwardly Snow's lecture has as its focus the division of intellectual life into two cultures. However on closer inspection it becomes evident that this is an essay that is much more concerned with society's uneasy relationship to its past and to its future. Snow is not so much interested in calling into question what he perceives as the arrogance and narrow-mindedness of the literary intellectual. His objection to the humanities is motivated by the historical association of this sphere of knowledge with the authority of the past. According to his schema of cultural life, 'scientists have the future in their bones' while 'traditional culture responds by wishing that the future did not exist'.[9] Snow takes the view that literary intellectuals are 'natural Luddites' who are bent on holding back the development of society.[10]

That Snow believed that literary intellectuals were out of touch with the problems of his times is well known. However, it is worth noting that he was also skeptical about the ability of scientific intellectuals to engage with what he saw as the practical problems facing the Britain of his time. His contempt for the 'pure scientist' reveals an implicit philistinism towards intellectual pursuits as such. 'I think it is only fair to say that most pure scientists have themselves been devastatingly ignorant of productive industry' he writes, before remarking that 'pure scientists have by and large been dim-witted about engineers and applied science'.[11] He is critical of pure scientists for their lack of interest in practical problems. Apparently the pure scientists who were his peers when he studied in Cambridge took it 'for granted that applied science was an occupation for second-rate minds'.[12] Snow's discussion of the relationship between pure and applied science is interesting because it reveals that his advocacy of the culture of the sciences is by no means free of contradictions. His advocacy of a future-oriented scientific culture lacks enthusiasm for the theoretical insights provided through disinterested scientific inquiry. From this perspective what he calls the 'new snobbism' of the pure scientist is no less of a threat than the old-fashioned elitism of the traditional literary intellectual. So what Snow upholds is not so much the culture of science but its application to deal with society's problems. His is a technocratic manifesto and his interest is focused on what works.

The reason why Snow objects to the influence of traditional culture is because he believes that attachment to the past undermines the capacity of society to adapt to change. And the reason why he castigates pure scientists is because of their refusal to engage with the practical problems facing society. From this standpoint both the upholder of traditional culture and the scientific quest for theoretical knowledge stand accused of the charge of being impractical and irrelevant to the changing needs of society. Pointing to Britain, he expressed his uncertainty about the country's capacity to adapt to the scientific revolution.[13] Snow's main pre-occupation is the capacity of Western society to adapt to changing conditions and incidentally to compete with the Soviet Union. His avowal of scientific culture is driven by the conviction that it provides the intellectual resources necessary for the modernisation of society.

The project of modernisation invariably demands that society break with the old ideas that are holding it back. Snow is no exception. Like many other technocractic modernisers—before and after him—Snow regarded education as a key site for waging a culture war against outdated ideas. If he were alive today he would have wholeheartedly approved the Blairite exhortation 'education, education, education'. Commenting on 'The Two Cultures', Snow argued that the transformation of education was the precondition for ensuring that Britain adapts to new circumstances. He conceded that 'changes in education will not, by themselves, solve our problems' but added that 'without those changes we shan't even realise what the problems are'.[14] As far as he was concerned, the reform of education was not simply a cultural matter: it directly effected the capacity of society to survive. He took the view that because of the continuing intellectual and cultural influence of the traditional elites Britain's global position was 'by a long way the most precarious'. Education was the most effective antidote to national decline. 'To say, we have to educate ourselves or watch a steep decline in our own lifetime, is about right' he argued.[15] On re-reading Snow it becomes clear that he was not simply interested in calling into question traditional intellectual pursuits. His lecture can be interpreted as a critique of intellectual pursuits that are not directly useful to society.

Although Snow would probably be disturbed by the lack of cultural affirmation for the authority of science, he would be delighted by the utilitarian turn adopted by policy-makers and educators. He would feel comfortable with the idea of the Knowledge Economy and the widely held view that above all education should help adapt society to a constantly changing world.

The fetishisation of change

Snow's rejection of the authority of the past is underpinned by an inflated perception of the impact of change on society. In line with the modernisers of his time, Snow concept-ualises change in a dramatic and mechanistic manner that exaggerates the novelty of the present moment. His outlook is shaped by an imagination that is so overwhelmed by the displacement of the old by the new that it often overlooks important dimensions of historical experience that may continue to be relevant to our lives. His discussion of the relationship between education and change is frequently overwhelmed by the fad of the moment and with the relatively superficial symptoms of new developments. So the apparent triumph of Soviet intellectual life appears to call into question the intellectual tradition that inspired the

Western imagination. From this perspective it is difficult to acknowledge the fact that the fundamental educational needs of students do not alter every time a new technology impacts on people's lives. And certainly the questions raised by Greek philosophy, Renaissance poetry, Enlightenment science or the novels of George Eliot continued to be relevant for students in Snow's time as much as in our Digital Age.

Experience shows that crisis narratives about the role of education tend to write off the legacy of the past as an outdated prejudice. Often change and social transformation is represented as a phenomenon that never happened previously. Like 'The Two Cultures', policy documents today continually repeat the refrain that 'we live in an age where the pace of change is more rapid than at any time in history'.[16] This rhetoric of unprecedented change is just that, rhetoric. It is not a conclusion that is based on a careful evaluation of the way societies have experienced change in the past. In a mechanistic way this approach divides the world into two periods: the past where either nothing or very little changed and the current moment when change is incessant.

Since the publication of 'The Two Cultures', the proposition that we live in an era of unprecedented change has acquired the character of a timeless formula which is constantly repeated as an argument for 'reforming' schooling and for altering how and what is taught in the classroom. 'But we should not forget why reform is right' stated Tony Blair in 1998 before reminding his audience yet again that 'the system must change because the world has changed beyond the recognition of Beveridge's generation'.[17] The world may have indeed changed since the publication of the Beveridge Report on education in 1944 but it is useful to recall that even in the early part of the twentieth century the refrain that 'the world has changed' was used to promote the cause of modernising schooling. Even before the outbreak of World War Two the fetishisation of change had a widespread presence in pedagogy. At the turn of the twentieth century, the renowned American philosopher of education John Dewey anticipated Blair's judgment about the magnitude of social and economic change. In an essay published in 1902 his argument for educational reforms rested on his diagnosis of rapid change, which led to the 'relaxation of social discipline and control' but also to the expansion of knowledge and technological innovation.[18]

During the succeeding decades the argument that the world was constantly changing became the foundational premise for educational reform. As an important study of the history of American school reforms noted, 'the case for changing the curriculum has been the same since the beginning of the twentieth century: society is changing, and the schools must change too'.[19] The pedagogue Michael Demiashkevich, who was a prominent critic of this approach, characterised the advocates of this dogma as neo-Heracliteans, who like the Greek philosopher Heraclitus insisted that change was the only constant in life. Heraclitus, who put forward the proposition that you could not step twice into same river, insisted that change was the only reality. Heraclitus's thesis of ceaseless change continues to enjoy the status of a foundational truth in much of modern pedagogy.

Demiashkevich asserted that the neo-Heraclitean perspective leads to 'an exaggerated degree of pedagogical chaos'.[20] Sadly, his prognosis of what he characterised as 'organised pedagogical anarchy' would turn out to be an accurate representation of events. By the 1960s an advocate of educational reform would self-consciously title his book *Technology and Change: The New Heraclitus*. Its author Donald

Schon, who was one of the leading early theorists of the idea of a Learning Society and of Life-Long Learning, noted that the 'loss of the stable state means that our society and all of its institutions are in a *continuous* processes of transformation'.[21] In 1972, when UNESCO issued its influential report *Learning To Be*, change was depicted as an autonomous and dramatic force that would render formal education increasingly obsolete and irrelevant. It predicted that 'progress in human knowledge and power, which has assumed such dizzying speed over the past 20 years, is only in its early stages' and that future prospects were at once 'exalting' and 'terrifying'.[22] Leading educationalists embraced the ideas contained in *Learning To Be* and concluded that schooling needed to be radically transformed if it were to keep up with the dizzying speed of change. According to one account: 'the central question to which we repeatedly return' is 'whether schools and colleges and universities can learn to adapt themselves rapidly enough to the changing world around them to avoid becoming, like the dinosaur, museum pieces'.[23]

Since the 1980s, but especially the 1990s, the attachment of educational policy to the fetish of change has acquired the form of an unquestioned dogma. Policy makers and educators self-consciously transmit a restless sense of confusion and disorder. 'We stand on the brink of a new age' cautioned former Secretary of State for Education and Employment David Blunkett. He continued his Heraclitean interpretation of the future by declaring that 'familiar certainties and old ways of doing things are disappearing'.[24] Through projecting a future of unrelenting uncertainty, British policy makers and their experts present the task of dealing with this chaos as the main challenge faced by schools. As Tom Bentley, a leading New Labour adviser, noted in 1998: 'the main task of a contemporary education system is to prepare its students for a world in which there is less order, less predictability and more chaos, where old solutions are running up against complex, apparently insurmountable challenges'.[25] By the turn of the twenty-first century the language of chaos and uncertainty served as a master frame through which British educationalists interpreted the issues facing the classroom. 'The fact is that wherever we look—science, history, management, politics— systems are giving way to chaos' asserted Michael Barber, another educational adviser to the New Labour Govern- ment.[26]

The dramatisation of change renders the past wholly irrelevant. If indeed we continually move from one 'new age' to another, then the institutions and practices of the past have little relevance for today. Indeed the ceaseless repetition of the proposition that the past is irrelevant serves to desensitise people from understanding the legacy of human development on their lives. Of course the constant reiteration of an argument—decade after decade—should at the very least lead an inquiring mind to question just how novel is the latest version of the 'new age'. However, every new generation of school-reformers imagines that they face an unprecedented period of perpetual socio-economic transformation. Their neo-Heraclitean perspective invariably associates change with chaos and uncertainty.

The idea of ceaseless change tends to turn it into an omnipotent, autonomous force that subjects human beings to its will. This is a force that turns the past into an irrelevant era and which demands that people learn to adapt and readapt to radically new experiences. From this standpoint human beings do not so much make history as adapt to powerful forces beyond their control.

Although the narrative of change has gained the status of an incontrovertible truth it is rarely supported by a conceptually elaborated argument. Indeed the dramatisation of change works mainly as a rhetorical device for signalling Western society's estrangement from the legacy of its past. In previous times the perception of an accelerating pace of change encouraged a disposition to embrace the past. In the nineteenth century many people—especially those of a conservative sensibility—looked to the past as a source of security in an alien world. Although many still seek security through an embrace of old traditions, the dominant tendency in Western societies is to flee from the past. This sensibility has been thoroughly assimilated into pedagogic policy which is continually fixated with novelty and innovation.

The association of the past with obsolescence is conveyed through a rhetorical strategy of naturalising change. Through the naturalisation of change any educational policy that seeks to draw on the cultural resources of the past is ruled out of the question. The objectification of change shuts down discussion of any alternative to the agenda of perpetual policy innovation. Staying still is not an option in a world where survival depends on the capacity to adapt. A phenomenon that works like an act of nature puts itself beyond debate. It can only be treated as a fact of life. From this standpoint the only educational policy that makes sense is one that can claim to keep up with change through helping people to adapt to it. 'In the discourses of professional development, change is said to be everywhere and we are urged to be prepared to deal with the uncertainties it engenders', contends a critical analysis of this rhetorical strategy.[27] It adds that 'the irony of this is that rhetorically change and uncertainty are positioned as certain'. In a world of uncertainty one fact is certain—the inevitability of yet more change.

Calls to modernise, reform and innovate education often tend to mystify their objectives. As is the case with 'The Two Cultures', the policies of modernisation are usually unspecific about the educational reform that they are trying to achieve. This is not surprising since the imperative to modernise or reform does not arise from problems that are integral to the system of education. Frequently such policies represent a response to issues that are entirely external to the workings of schools and colleges. For example, today the call to personalise learning is not acclaimed as an innovation that is chiefly justified on the grounds that 'impersonal' learning impedes the work of schools. This 'innovation' is offered as a solution to problems that have been identified outside the school gate. A report promoting personalising learning points to the need for schools to respond to an 'ethnically and socially diverse society', 'far greater access to, and reliance on, technology', a 'knowledge-based economy', 'demanding employers', 'sharper focus on sustainability' and—arguably one development that's integral to education —'complex pathways through education and training'.[28]

As in Snow's time, calls for educational reform are often couched in a dramatic language that appeals to the instinct of economic survival. Warnings about the economic consequences of being left adrift in an increasingly complex and technologically innovative world provide the main rationale for reform. According to a study of the 'epidemic' of reforms, the necessity for new education policy is 'largely cast in economic terms and particularly in relation to the preparation of a workforce and competition with other countries'.[29] That is why the problems associated with schooling are frequently interpreted as a threat to economic welfare and prosperity rather than to the intellectual life of society.[30]

No doubt Snow would be pleased that contemporary culture no longer merely regards adaptability as a useful attribute of personhood but as a defining characteristic of a competent individual. That is why policy statements often convey the message that education is not so much about the teaching of a particular subject but the cultivation of the habit of adaptability. The capacity to adapt requires people to change so that they can develop the ability to respond to new developments. Donald Schon argued that children need to develop an 'ethic of change' in order to cope with the fluid reality they inhabit.[31] Consequently what's important is not what people know but the possession of the mental capacity to adapt and respond to new circumstances. That's one reason why behaviour management and therapeutic techniques have become part of the landscape of schooling. 'Effective change in a field as dependent on human inter-action as education requires millions of people to change their behaviour' argued David Blunkett in 1997.[32] That is why the ascendancy of therapeutic education and the institutionalisation of behaviour management represents one of the most significant development in contemporary Anglo-American education.

There is little doubt that Western intellectual life continues to be divided between different cultures. But the tension between the humanities and science outlined in 'The Two Cultures' has become overwhelmed by a fundamental confusion about the very meaning of education. The narrow instrumentalist ethos conveyed through Snow's lecture has acquired a powerful cultural influence. This development is not surprising. The growing tendency to distance society from its past and the fetishisation of change has undermined the foundation on which a forward-looking intellectual life can be constructed. A one-sided emphasis on the imperative of adaptability fails to understand that it is only through the assimilation of our cultural and scientific inheritance that society can possess the intellectual resources with which to engage with the problems of the future. What Snow could not quite grasp was that to answer the questions that have not yet been asked we need to make the best possible use of our historic legacy.

Notes

Robert Whelan: Any Culture At All Would Be Nice

1   Snow, C.P., *The Two Cultures*, Cambridge: Cambridge University Press, 2007, p. 11.

2   Snow, 2007, pp. 29-30.

3   Snow, 2007, p. 7.

4   Snow, 2007, p. 39.

5   Snow, 2007, p. 40.

6   Snow, 2007, p. 36.

7   Snow, 2007, p. 42.

8   Snow, 2007, pp. 47&50.

9   Snow, 2007, p. 45.

10 *Encounter*, June and July 1959.

11 Snow, C.P., 'The Two Cultures: A Second Look', added to the Cambridge University Press edition of *The Two Cultures* from 1964 onwards. P. 54 of the 2007 edition cited above.

12 Leavis, F.R., *Two Cultures? The Significance of C.P. Snow*, London: Chatto and Windus, 1962.

13 Leavis, 1962, pp.10, 11, 15, 16, 18.

14 Trilling, L., 'The Leavis/Snow Controversy', first published in *Commentary*, June 1962, then reprinted in *The Moral Obligation to be Intelligent: Selected Essays*, New York: Farrar, Straus and Giroux, 2001, p. 406.

15 Collini, S., Introduction to Snow, 2007, p. xxxii.

16 Leavis, 1962, pp. 12, 13, 19.

17 Leavis, 1962, p. 29.

18 Quoted in Dean, P., 'The Last Critic? The Importance of F.R. Leavis' in *Counterpoints: Twenty-Five Years of The New Criterion on Culture and the Arts*, Chicago: Ivan R. Dee, 2007, p. 256.

19 Snow, P., *Stranger and Brother: A Portrait of C.P. Snow*, London: Macmillan, 1982, p. 143.

20 Snow, P., 1982, p. 164.

21 Holland, M. and Hart-Davis, R. (eds), *The Complete Letters of Oscar Wilde*, London: Fourth Estate, p. 769.

22 Trilling, L., 1962.

23 Arnold, M., 'Literature and Science' (1882), reprinted in Super, R.H. (ed.), *The Complete Prose Works of Matthew Arnold*, vol. X, Ann Arbor, 1974, pp. 52-73.

24 Huxley, T.E., 'Science and Culture' (1880) reprinted in Huxley, T.E., *Science and Education: Essays*, London, 1893, pp. 134-59.

25 Smith, A., *An Inquiry into the Nature and Causes of the Wealth of Nations*, Book V.

26 Quoted in Tallis, R., *Newton's Sleep: Two Cultures and Two Kingdoms*, London: Macmillan, 1995, p. 11.

27 Coleridge, S.T., *The Statesman's Manual or The Bible the Best Guide to Political Skill and Foresight: A lay sermon addressed to the higher classes of society, with an appendix, containing comments and essays connected with the study of inspired writing*, London, 1816. The words quoted occur in Appendix A, p. 38 in White, R.J. (ed.), *Political Tracts of Wordsworth, Coleridge and Shelley*, Cambridge: Cambridge University Press, 1953.

28 Holmes, R., *The Age of Wonder: How the Romantic generation discovered the beauty and terror of science*, London: HarperCollins, 2008, p. 319.

29 'Entire books have been dedicated to following through the minatory influence of Frankenstein's Creature … suffice it to note here that the current discussion of GM crops—undoubtedly vital to sustain global harvests and reduce dependency on crop spraying— often refers to them as "Frankenstein foods" … and that the *Guardian's* excellent column "Bad Science" has an image of Frankenstein's monster as its logo.' Holmes, 2008, p. 457n.

30 The 'ingenious gentleman' was William Whewell, from whose account of this meeting in the *Quarterly Review* the quotation is

taken. *Quarterly Review*, 51, 1834, pp. 54-68. Quoted in Holmes, 2008, p. 449.

31 Moore, J., *Portrait of Elmbury* (1945) in *The Brensham Trilogy*, Oxford: Oxford University Press, 1985, p. 53.

32 Speech delivered by Sir Andrew Huxley on the occasion of his ninetieth birthday, reprinted Trinity College Cambridge Annual Record 2007-2008, p. 79.

33 Snow, 2007, p. 18.

34 Snow, 2007, pp. 61, 86.

35 Perks, D., 'What is Science Education For?' in Whelan, R. (*ed.*), *The Corruption of the Curriculum*, Civitas: London, 2007, p. 23.

36 *The Twenty First Century Science Pilot Evaluation Report*, UYSEG and Nuffield Foundation, February 2007.

37 Dr Robert Coe of Durham University's Centre for Evaluation (CEM) and Monitoring used independent data to show how this allowed pupils of similar standards to achieve different results over the years. A student who scored 45 (just below the average) on the YELLIS test could expect to achieve D grades in French, Maths and History at GCSE in 1996, but by 2005 would be receiving C grades; enough to push a number of students into achieving the five grades at A*-C government 'benchmark'. Taking an average of 26 subjects, pupils of the same YELLIS standard could generally expect to achieve around half a grade higher in 2005 than they could in 1996. Robert Coe used the International Test of Developed Abilities to compare the actual attainment of A-level pupils from year to year with their paper qualifications. Taking an average of 40 A-level subjects, he found that those scoring 50 per cent on the ITDA test in 1997 would tend to achieve low C grades, but by 2005 were achieving low B grades. ('Changes in standards at GCSE and A-Level: Evidence from ALIS and YELLIS,' Coe, R., CEM Centre, Durham University, April 2007.)

38 According to analysis of income inequality and poverty in countries belonging to the Organisation for Economic Cooperation and Development (OECD) the UK is performing poorly on social mobility. Whilst Denmark and Australia, for example, have very

high levels of social mobility, the UK, together with Italy and United States, are amongst those countries with the very lowest levels of mobility. Earnings in the UK have also seen an increase of inequality, with the wage gap having widened by 20 per cent since 1985. (*Growing Unequal? Income Distribution and Poverty in OECD Countries*, 'Income inequality and poverty rising in most OECD countries', Organisation for Economic Cooperation and Development, October 2008.)

39 The information for the University of Oxford is as follows:

Admissions Rounds	% of UK applications from state schools	% of UK offers to state school applicants
2001-2007	57.6	53.56
1991-2000	53.7	50.04
1982-1990	54.4	49.40
1970-1981	67.4	63.80
1964-1965	57.6	59.20

40 Trilling, 1962, pp. 421 & 422.

41 Snow, 2007, p. 26.

42 Simon, J., *The Ultimate Resource 2*, Princeton New Jersey: Princeton University Press, 1996, p. 261.

43 Taverne, D., *The March of Unreason: Science, Democracy and the New Fundamentalism*, Oxford: Oxford University Press, p. 186.

Raymond Tallis: The Eunuch at the Orgy

1 Snow, C.P., *The Two Cultures and the Scientific Revolution*, Cambridge: Cambridge University Press, 1959.

2 Leavis, F.R., *Two Cultures: The Significance of C.P. Snow*, London: Chatto & Windus, 1962.

3 Norris, C., 'Introduction' to Bell, M., *F.R. Leavis*, London: Routledge, Critics of the Twentieth Century, 1988, p. vii.

4   On how critics deal with the threat of *Kritikerschuld*, see Tallis, R., *In Defence of Realism*, London: Edward Arnold, 1988; 2nd edn, London: Ferrington, 1994, especially pp. 159-70.

5   Williams, R., *Culture and Society 1780-1950*, London: Chatto & Windus, 1958.

6   Trilling, L., *Beyond Culture*, London: Penguin, 1967.

7   Norris, 'Introduction' to Bell, *F.R. Leavis*, 1988.

8   Appleyard, B., *Understanding the Present*, London: Picador, 1992.

9   Nash, C., *Narrative in Culture*, London: Routledge, 1990.

10 Maynard Smith, J., *The Theory of Evolution*, London: Penguin, 1975.

11 Gross, A., *The Rhetoric of Science*, Harvard University Press, 1990. Gross's book is demolished by John Durant's article (to which the present discussion is indebted), 'Is Science a Social Invention?', in *The Times Literary Supplement*, 15 March 1991, p. 19.

12 Appendix F to the Challenger Report 'Personal Observations on the Reliability of the Shuttle', quoted in Feynman, R., *What Do You Care What Other People Think?*, W.W. Norton, 1988.

13 For a further discussion of the relationship between magic and science and the attempt to reduce the latter to the former—or indeed to show that magic is superior to science—see my *Enemies of Hope*, Macmillan, 1997, revised edn, 1999.

14 Kuhn, T., *The Structure of Scientific Revolutions*, Chicago: University of Chicago Press, 2nd edn, 1970.

15 Wolpert, L., *The Unnatural Nature of Science*, London: Faber, 1992.

16 The relationship between the truth of science and the fact that it works is addressed by Paul Valéry in his dialogue, *Idée Fixe*, translated by David Paul, New York: Bollingen/Pantheon, 1965:

   —If I set about adding up what we know, I find the gains are illusory… If, on the other hand, I look at what we can do—at mankind's acquisition of real power over a century and a half, then…
   —But how can you separate this fictive knowledge, this substantial power, the one from the other? (p. 100)

—I mean consider simply the increase in power. All the rest, theories, hypotheses, analogies—mathematical or otherwise—is both indispensable and provisional. What remains as capital is simply the powers of action upon things, the new achievements, the recipes... Science, translated in technology, works. (p. 101)

The implication is that theories may come and go but their enduring remnant is the recipes, the powers, the achievements they leave behind. Whatever the fate of quantum theory, nothing can take away the silicon chip, and all the devices based on it and the transformation of history and human life that resulted from them. A couple of points may be made against this separation of the *truth* from the *power* of science-based technology:

(a) As pointed out in the text, although theories are often superseded, much from the past, and distant past, of science survives indefinitely. The present of science is built on its past: successful theories and enduringly true facts will be invisible inasmuch as they will be taken for granted as part of the accepted body of knowledge.

(b) It would be an improbable coincidence if a theory that accounts for more of the known facts than any rival theory, predicts novel facts, brings together many other facts and postulates or supports practical technologies, were totally unrelated to what is actually the case 'out there'. The theories and the recipes cannot, therefore, be entirely unrelated.

Even so, the relationship between the truth of science and the success of the technology based upon it is not straightforward. For this reason, it deserves better treatment than the superficial, inaccurate and envy-motivated accounts of the social scientists.

Frank Furedi: Re-reading C.P. Snow

1   Zieger, R., '"Uncle Sam Wants You... To Go Shopping": A Consumer Society Responds to National Crisis, 1957-2001', *Canadian Review of American Studies*, vol. 34, no. 1, 2004, p. 87.

2   Zieger, '"Uncle Sam Wants You... To Go Shopping"', *Canadian Review of American Studies*, 2004, p. 91.

3   Snow, C.P., *The Two Cultures*, Cambridge: Cambridge University Press, 2007, p. 50.

4   Snow (2007) p. 14.

5   See Robert Whelan's comments in the Introduction to this collection of essays.

6   For a discussion of these trends, see Furedi, F., *Where Have All the Intellectuals Gone?*, Continuum Press: London, 2006.

7   See 'Traditional subjects go in schools shake-up', *The Times*; 8 December 2008.

8   White, J., 'Towards an aims-led curriculum', QCA; www.qca.org.uk/futures/.

9   Snow (2007) p. 11.

10 Snow (2007) p. 22.

11 Snow (2007) pp. 32 & 33.

12 Snow (2007) p. 32.

13 Snow (2007) p. 38.

14 Snow (2007) pp. 99-100.

15 Snow (2007) pp. 39 & 40.

16 Qualifications and Curriculum Authority, *A Curriculum For The Future*, QCA: London, 2005, p. 4.

17 Cited in Ball, S., *The Education Debate*, Policy Press: Bristol, 2008, p. 11.

18 Dewey, J., 'The School as a Social Center' in Dewey, J., (first published 1902) *The Child And The Curriculum*, University of Chicago Press: Chicago, 1956.

19 Ravitch, D., *Left Back: A Century of Failed School Reforms*, New York: Simon & Schuster, 2000, p. 335.

20 Cited in Ravitch, 2000, p. 292.

21 Schon, D., *Technology and Change: The New Heraclitus*, Oxford: Pergamon Press, 1967, p. 28.

22 UNESCO, *The World of Education Today and Tomorrow—Learning to Be*, Paris: UNESCO, 1972, pp. 90-91.

23 Coombs, P., *The World Crisis In Education: The View From The Eighties*, New York: Oxford University Press, 1985, p. 250.

24 'Foreword by David Blunkett, 'The Learning Age: A renaissance for a new Britain'; http://www.lifelonglearning.co.uk/greenpaper/summary.pdf

25 Bentley, T., *Learning Beyond the Classroom: Education for a Changing World*, London: Routledge, 1998, p. 177.

26 Barber, M., *The Learning Game: Arguments For An Education Revolution*, Indigo: London, 1997, p. 160.

27 Edwards, R. & Nicoll, K., 'Expertise, competence and reflection in the rhetoric of professional development', *British Educational Research Journal*, vol. 32, no. 1, 2006, p. 118.

28 *2020 Vision: Report of the Teaching and Learning in 2020*, Review Group, London, 2006, p. 8.

29 Levin, B., 'An Epidemic of Education Policy: (what) can we learn from each other?', *Comparative Education;* vol. 34, no. 2, 1998, p. 131.

30 These points are developed in my forthcoming *Lost In Education*, London: Continuum Press: London, 2009.

31 Schon, *Technology and Change*, 1967, p. 217.

32 See DfEE, *Excellence in Schools*, 1997, p. 12.